Dreamboats & Milestones: Cars of the '50s

by Chris Halla

MODERN AUTOMOTIVE SERIES

TAB BOOKS Inc.

BLUE RIDGE SUMMIT, PA. 17214

FIRST EDITION

FIRST PRINTING

Printed in the United States of America

Library of Congress Cataloging in Publication Data

Halla, Chris.
Dreamboats & milestones.

Includes index.
1. Automobiles—United States—History. I. Title.
TL23.H34 629.2'222'0973 80-28328
ISBN 0-8306-9625-3
ISBN 0-8306-2065-6 (pbk.)

Cover photo courtesy of Mike Carbonelle

Contents

Acknowledgments

Appreciation is due to the following individuals and organizations, without whom this book could not have been completed.

First, the many car clubs who helped with technical and production data, photos and insights on the character of their favorite cars.

Ron McQueeney, Director of Photography for Indianapolis Motor Speedway Corporation, for providing info and photos on ten years of Indy Pace Cars.

Bill McBride, who provided a wealth of information on contemporary advertising.

Don Adams of Henry Ford Museum and Greenfield Village, and the staff of the Ford Archives for opening up to me and many other researchers that great storehouse of knowledge, the Edison Institute.

The Society of Automotive Historians, from whom it would seem nearly all automotive knowledge can be gained.

The very cooperative P.R. and Archival people of American Motors Corporation; Buick Motor Division, GM; Cadillac Division of GM; Chevrolet Motor Division, GM; Chrysler Corporation; Dodge; Ford Motor Company; General Motors Division, GM; Oldsmobile Division, GM; Pontiac Motor Division, National Automobile Dealer's Association and Motor Vehicle Manufacturer's Association.

My mother and father; Gayle, Donna, Floyd and Mary Sue for their encouragement. Verley Paulson, Carl Hazelwood and Terry Gaffney for their knowledge of things mechanical and their willingness to apply that knowledge to my various machines. Gary Busha, my best critic. Finally, but most of all, Janet and Joshua for their unbending patience, and Rachel for the final push.

Introduction

To some members of the automotive fraternity, there just isn't anything prettier than a rake-and-ramblin' Thirties classic. Others prefer pioneer brass, Twenties boxes or the everlasting tanks of the best forgotten Forties. For a few, only the over-powered Sixties machines will do.

But give me one of those great, gaudy bombs from the Fifties every time. Yes sir, when I fly, I want to fly down time's highway in something more than nice. I want to go in something nifty. Give me fins that point to heaven and a two-tone paint job; an automatic tranny and short stroke V-8. That's the car for me. And judging from all the activity taking place lately in the auto hobby, I'm not alone; in fact, there's more trading activity in Fifties cars than in all the rest put together.

The Fifties was the decade of James Dean and Marilyn Monroe, Elvis Presley and Fats Domino, "I Like Ike" and Joe McCarthy. Wyatt Earp, the Mavericks and Cheyenne Bodie were riding the video range. The Braves were still in Milwaukee. In the automotive industry, it was a decade of finny flamboyance. Chrome was king.

For car enthusiasts, the Fifties have come back to life. The new rule of thumb is, "if it was made between 1949 and 1960, it's collectible." Among these cars, there are four categories: The "bread-and-butter" cars that are attracting the attention, of enthusiasts who want a Fifties car and have very little money to spend; the "nice" cars, carrying a touch of the magic Fifties flair; the milestones, recognized as such by the Milestone Car Society for their mechanical and/or stylistic innovations; and the dreamboats, the cars that caught everybody's eye back then and are still doing it today. Many of the dreamboats of the Fifties fall into the milestone category and vice versa. It's in the last two categories that the hottest activity is taking place.

In the pages that follow, you will find historical background for the dreamboats and milestones of the Fifties; comments on their good points and bad points; and their degree of collectibility. You'll learn how to go about finding one, how to buy one and keep it up, and finally, how to sell that dreamboat when a better catch comes along.

You will find a price guide for the cars in question; a list of clubs for Fifties enthusiasts; resources, bibliography and other information you'll need to obtain and enjoy the great cars from the age of chrome.

A note on what isn't included is necessary here. As I said earlier, only the most desirable cars are included. If you can't find the car of your dreams or, more likely, can't afford it, don't give up. Often, the next car in line will yield the same rewards as old number one. Simply keep in mind that convertibles, sport coupes, hardtops and coupes (roughly in that order) are the most sought after body styles. Sedans, especially the four-door variety, are the least so. Always buy the high dollar model. There are exceptions, but it's best to follow these simple rules until you have a firm grasp of hobby markets.

Chris Halla

Chapter 1
General Motors

There is no more fitting place to begin this survey of the Fifties than with General Motors. The list of GM cars that fall into the dreamboat and milestone category is at least twice as long as that of any other American manufacturer. From this list comes the 1955-57 Chevy—perhaps the most popular of all Fifties collectibles—and the super extravagant, high-finned Cadillacs. From the GM lineup, the enthusiast can pick just about any kind of car he wants, knowing full well that it is a car that somebody else in the hobby would give his eye teeth for.

BUICK

Huge, powerhouse V-8's and some very trendy styling mark the Buicks of the Fifties. Performance, quality and style indicative of the times are factors that sold Buicks then, and make them popular with collectors today (Fig. 1-1).

The 1951 Buick Roadmaster convertible is powered by the proven, valve-in-head, straight eight of 320 CID. The smooth, but unexciting Dynaflow transmission is standard here. Current prices for these early Fifties grease machines will run from one grand to as high as $7,500. That's not cheap, but it's still a good buy for the enthusiast who wants a flashy pre-1955 Buick.

Probably the most incredible Buick of the decade is the limited edition, 1953 Skylark sport convertible, based on the Roadmaster series, minus portholes. Buick made 1,690 of these

Fig. 1-1. 1950 Buick Roadmaster convertible. Style remained almost identical from '49 through '52.

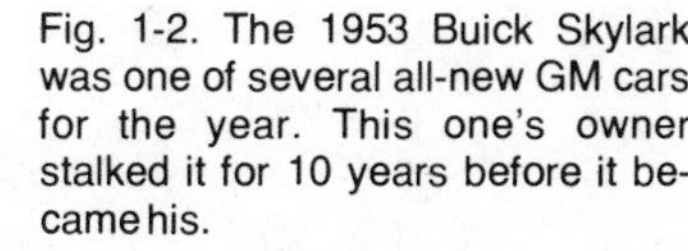

Fig. 1-2. The 1953 Buick Skylark was one of several all-new GM cars for the year. This one's owner stalked it for 10 years before it became his.

Detroit customs at a price to the consumer of $5,000. This, plus the car's instant eye appeal made them a natural with the high-visibility crowd (Fig. 1-2).

Styling isn't everything though, and mechanically the '53 Buicks have something going for them too. For example, a 12-volt electrical system, power steering and an ohv V-8, boasting 322 cubes and 188 horsepower at 4,000 rpm. A four-barrel carburetor feeds fuel to the engine.

The Skylark started life as a Harley Earl styling exercise to create a Golden Anniversary automobile that would have wide appeal in a marketplace where sports car were adored, but not purchased in large quantities. The result is a sporty, luxurious personal car (Fig. 1-3).

The Skylark is a big GM convertible after chopping and channeling. The windshield is four inches lower than standard Buicks of the same vintage. The belt line is lowered. The rear fender line is notched. Rear wheel wells are cut out in a circular fashion to match those up front. Instead of plain wheels and hubcaps, tires are wrapped around Borrani wire wheels with knock offs.

In July of 1977, I paid $5,500 for a brand new car. One of the fellows I worked with went out and bought a '53 Skylark at the same time for $3,500. That bright red Buick was so stunning that I immediately offered to trade my new machine for it. The offer was just as quickly declined. Today that Buick would pay back the original cost of my new car and provide several thousands more as a bonus (Fig. 1-4).

The good news, for enthusiasts willing and able to part with the big bucks Skylarks are going for, is that they promise to keep going up. Even if you pay a little more than the car is worth now, it is likely to pay off in as little as a year. (This is something to keep in mind with all of the dreamboats and milestones we will be talking about).

For model year 1954, the Skylark reappeared, though in a less pleasing form. In years past, collectors believed the '54 model to be worth more than the '53, because only 836 '54's were built. This is one of the those cases where basing the desirability of a car on scarcity alone failed to hold true. Today, the 1953 Skylark is worth a couple thousand more than the '54 (Fig. 1-5).

The 1954 Skylark is a much less interesting car, based on the Century body. Again, there are no portholes. Wheel wells are wide open, as in 1953, but this time they are elongated, creating a

Fig. 1-3. More than anything, the '53 Skylark is a custom job.

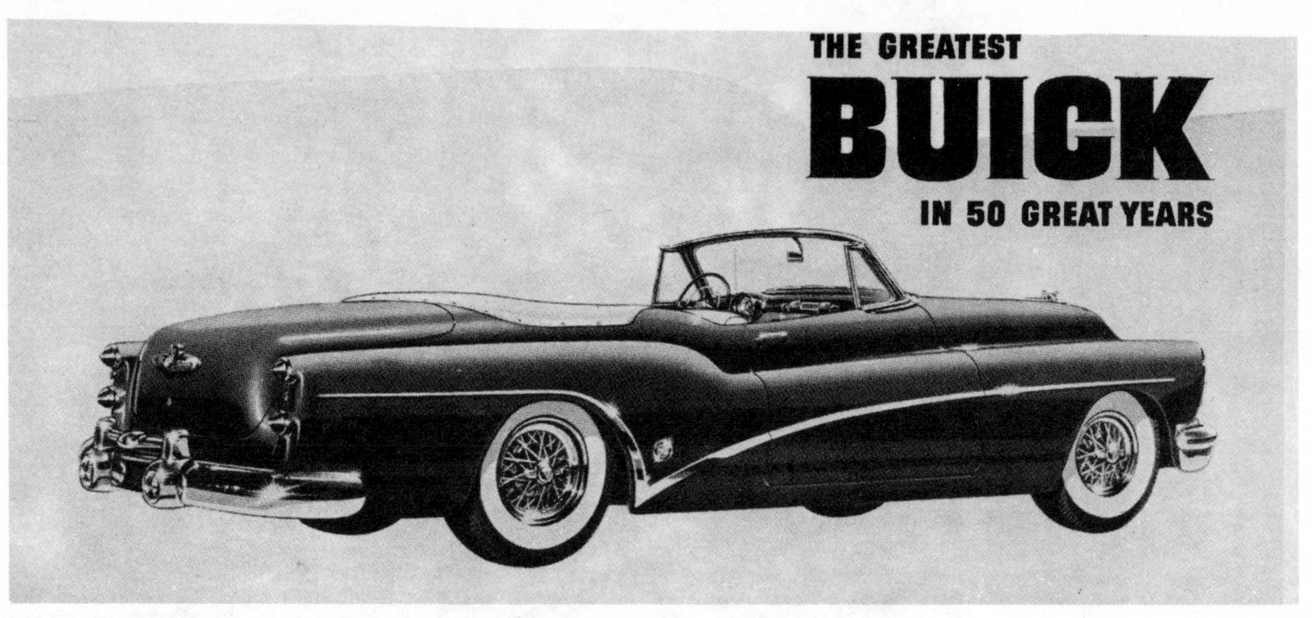

Fig. 1-4. Buick billed the new Skylark as "the greatest Buick" in 50 years.

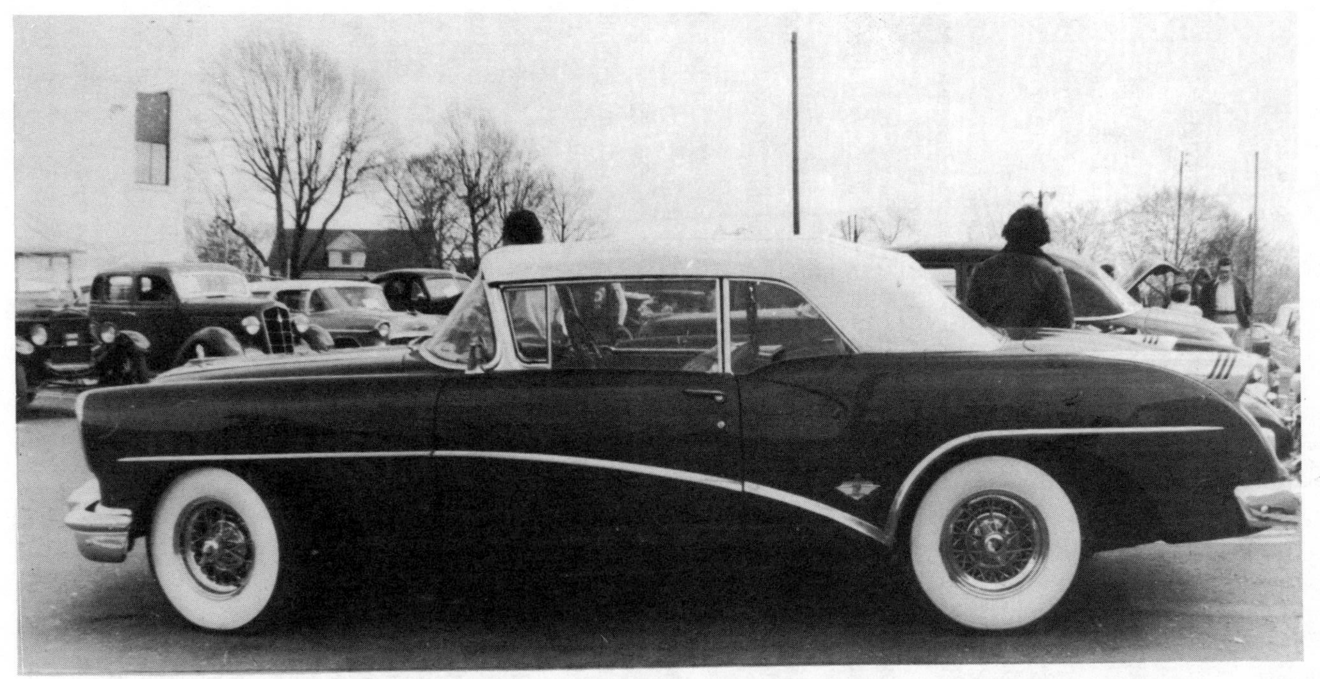

Fig. 1-5. The 1954 Skylark is rarer than the '53, but not quite as good looking. Even at a little higher price, the '53 is a better buy.

rather bizarre effect. This is topped off by a sloping decklid and heavy, tacked-on chrome tail fins and taillight housings. Powerplant is a 200 horsepower V-8. It sold for $4,485, new (Fig. 1-6).

The entire Buick line had been restyled in 1954 with a boxier body and wraparound windshield. 1955 and 1956 models followed the same basic style with slight modifications.

What came of all this minor modification was the 1956 Roadmaster convertible, the most outstanding Buick since the Golden Anniversary Skylark. The '56 Roadmaster has a powerful, windswept look, and Buicks of 1956 were in fact more powerful than they had ever been before.

Powerplant in the Roadmaster convertible is a 352 CID V-8, capable of zero-to-60 in less than 11 seconds, and 115 miles per hour. Front suspension, rear axle and a variety of other chassis improvements were new for 1956. Over 4,000 of these goin' machines were built, which means a number of them probably are still around for enthusiasts today.

Buick suffered from sales problems in 1956, in spite of some excellent automobiles. 1957 was better, though not what the boys in the front office had hoped for.

What Buick did to improve its fortunes in 1958, was Buick did the same thing that so many other American automobile manufacturers were doing to improve their fortunes in '58; sharpening those fins, piling on the chrome, doubling the headlights. What resulted is just what you might expect, a car singular in its excessive bad taste. The portholes are gone, replaced by an almost completely chrome-covered front end and garnish tail fins. The over-sized 1958 Buicks are heavier by 400 pounds than the Buicks that opened the decade.

Even the newly introduced air suspension option (for which few buyers opted) and their exceptional speed couldn't save these chrome-laden tanks; what Buick didn't do to kill its own sales, the 1958 recession did.

So, you might wonder, what possible reason could there be for including any 1958 Buick in a list of dreamboats and milestones? Glad you asked.

The 1958 Buick Limited convertible is a car that, like the 1956 Hudson Hornet Hollywood hardtop in all of its three tone splendor, is a dreamboat because of its excesses. This is one of those rare cars that is as ugly as sin, but draws ooh's and ah's wherever it is seen. Among the '58 Buicks, the Limited convertible is one of the most excessive and the most sought after by collectors, investors and enthusiasts today.

Fig. 1-6. A 200 horsepower mill and twin turbine Dynaflow make the 1954 Skylark as much hot rod as custom machine.

Model year 1959 Buicks were entirely new. Tail fins are much more pronounced on the '59's than on their predecessors, but the look is smooth and flowing. The overall shape of the car is one of an automobile well-prepared for the rocket age. The old, traditional Buick names are gone, replaced by LeSabre, Invicta, Electra and Electra 225.

The most outstanding 1959 Buick is the stunning Electra 225 convertible, made even more special to enthusiasts by virtue of its having been chosen as the official Pace Car of the 1959 Indianapolis 500 (Fig. 1-7). Pace Car status is a thing which cannot be underestimated with automobile enthusiasts. There is a magic at work here which is quite unexplainable. I suspect this adoration for Indy Pace Cars is based on the assumption by enthusiasts that, if it was chosen to be a Pace Car, then it must be something special. At any rate, Pace Cars are premium cars when bought and sold.

Among the new mechanical developments that showed up on the Electra 225 and elsewhere in the 1959 Buick line are power steering and brakes, air conditioning and (unsuccessfully again) air suspension in the rear. Power for the Electra came from a 401 cube, 325 horsepower V-8. The value of these cars is climbing slowly though steadily, with those most closely resembling the '59 Indy Pace Car the standouts.

With Buicks, as with all high interest automobiles, when a convertible can't be had, a hardtop or coupe is the next logical choice for a car that is likely to attract the desire of enthusiasts and therefore escalate in value during the time you own and enjoy it. It should be noted though, that when it comes to Buicks of the Fifties, convertibles are considerably more desirable than their stationary topped relations.

CADILLAC

To say that in recent years—the last 20 if you apply a long hard look—Cadillac has lost the lion's share of its flash, would be an understatement. One must go a step further and say that Cadillacs since 1960 have, for the most part, become very boring. Compared to their predecessors of the Fifties, the newest Cadillacs seem like little more than over-priced Chevys. So why not buy a perfectly good Chevy and save yourself a few shillings?

But in the Fifties, by golly, Cadillac was building automobiles. Some are beautiful, some grotesque. Some offer neat sports car handling, others drive like clapped-out Sherman tanks. But, damn it, they have character. There isn't a Cadillac produced between

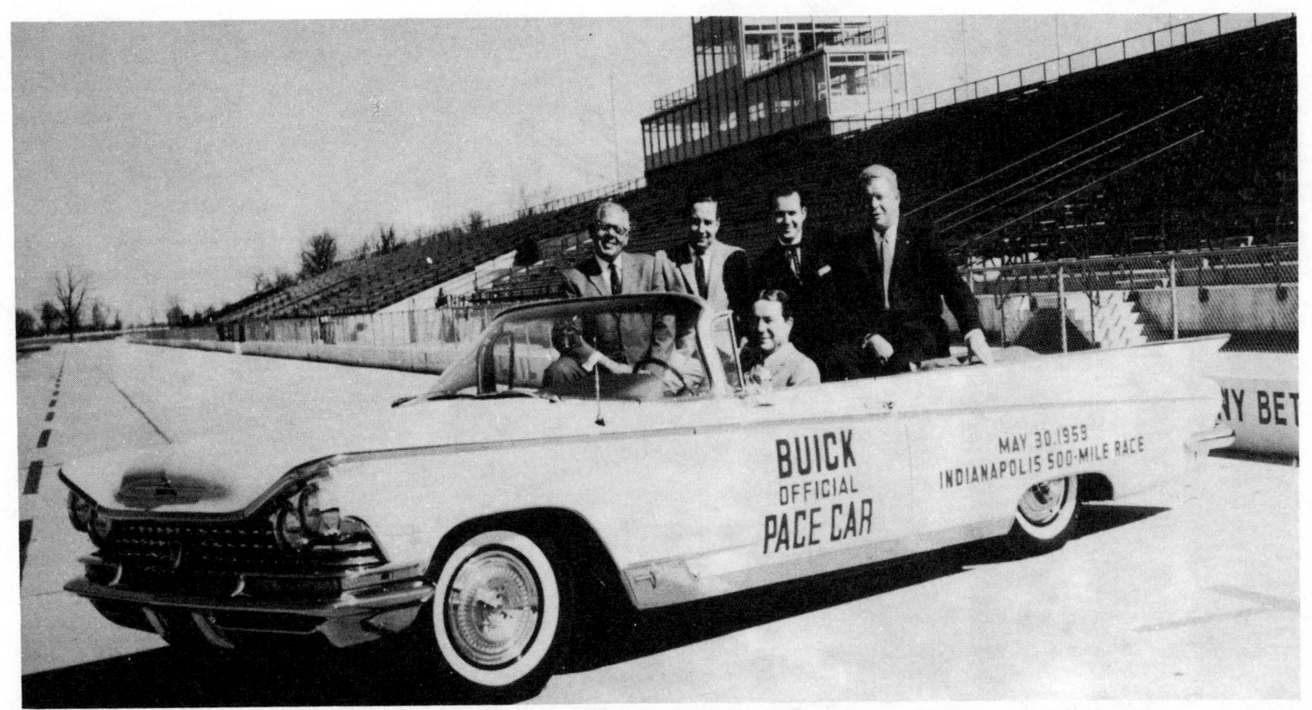

Fig. 1-7. The 1959 Buick that paced Indy that year. Behind the wheel is Tony Hulman. The other four gents are local Buick dealers.

1949 and 1960 that won't turn heads anywhere you take it. Every one of them has some attraction for collectors. Our survey will cover only the most desirable models, but if you find one in good condition that's not listed, it is more than likely worth having.

Let's begin with the 1950 Series 62 convertible, with its new-for-the-decade pop top. Of Cadillac's 104,000 total 1950 production, nearly 7,000 were Series 62 convertible coupes. Recent estimates suggest that only about 40 of these babies survive. My guess would be a little higher than that, possibly twice as many. The point is, however, that they are rare. A current price tag in the $10,000 range is reflective of that.

The '50 convertible rests on a 126-inch wheelbase. The engine is a V-8 of 331 CID with hydraulic valve lifters. The transmission is Hydra-Matic.

Again, in model years 1951 and '52, the Series 62 convertible is the hot number. In fact, both of these years are valued higher than the '50 in current collector circles.

Of these two, go for the '52. Current values are very close, but years down the road may see more separation. In 1952, Cadillac got power steering, power binders, dual range Hydra-Matic—which would sit in third gear forever if you wanted it to—and a progressive linkage, Rochester four-barrel carburetor.

In 1953, the first-ever Cadillac Eldorado burst upon the scene. Priced at $7,750, the Eldorado became, far and away, the most expensive car of the year. Like the Buick Skylark of the same vintage, the Eldorado was a special edition. Some critics say that this is where Cadillac's age of opulence really got rolling (Fig. 1-8). I guess that confirms that beauty is in the eyes of the beholder, because I think this great, hulking animal of a machine is quite stylish. Considering the fact that one of these Eldorados is worth roughly $17,000 to today's collectors, it looks like I'm not the only one who likes it.

At $2,000 more than the next highest priced Cadillac, some extra luxury could be expected in the Eldorado. Buyers, I suspect, were not disappointed. There is a custom interior, with a number of cloth and leather combos available; a metal boot to cover the top when in repose; a Hydramatic or Dynaflow automatic transmission; a cutdown, wrap-around windshield; wire wheels and standard power steering.

There are plenty of Cadillacs from the Fifties available to collectors today, and as I said, all of them are collectible. However, if I could own any one I wanted, my choice would be the 1953

Fig. 1-8. The hulking, highly sought after, 1953 Cadillac Eldorado convertible.

Cadillac Eldorado convertible. As far as I'm concerned, it is one of the two or three most outstanding cars produced in the decade.

Cadillacs of 1954 were restyled. Most noticeably, the bulging lines of recent model years levelled out, giving a more sweeping look overall. Again, the Eldorado convertible is the hot number (Fig. 1-9).

For contemporary buyers, the '54 version was priced at only $5,738. That ain't exactly cheap, but it's a lot cheaper than the same model in 1953. While the dollars decreased, the wheelbase increased by three inches to 129 inches.

The Eldo still carried fancy wire wheels. The metal convertible top cover of 1953 became fiberglass in 1954. Power steering, brakes and seats were standard equipment. The interior is a little less extravagant. A bright-work trim panel appears on the lower rear fender. The car is powered by a 331 CID engine with 230 horses.

Because of a few cuts here and there, resulting in the lower price while maintaining pretty high quality, the 1954 Eldo sold 2,150 copies. Top value today is around $12,000—some $5,000 less than the class of '53.

For 1955 all Cadillacs got a minor facelift. The Eldorado, though, got a little bit more. The tailfins grew from a small hump, like the one on the back of a baby shark, to a sharp, chrome-edged affair, perched above dual taillights. Those beautiful wires disappeared and were replaced by disc wheels, called Sabre Spokes by Cadillac. Fender skirts went bye-bye, opening up the wheelwells. The chrome trim from the rear panel moved up to the top of the doors (Fig. 1-10). In the engine compartment, the Eldorado got its own power unit, 270 horses worth. The number of Eldos produced in 1955 was nearly double that of '54.

In 1956, the Eldorado Seville became a coupe. The new high-dollar convertible was christened Eldorado Biarritz. They both sold for $6,501 new.

Both new top-of-the-line Cadillacs sailed down the road, under the power of a 365 CID mill of 305 horsepower. The neatest part of that powerplant is a dual four-barrel setup guaranteed to make gas station owners smile. In common for the two models are Sabre Spoke wheels, larger rear bumper housings, larger oval exhaust ports and, for buyers who wanted it, gold trim on the grille mesh and wheels. The biggest difference, other than their tops (by the way, the Seville has a fabric covered roof), is the way they sold. The Seville outsold the Biarritz almost two-to-one.

Fig. 1-9. The Cadillac look at its best: 1954 Eldorado Special Convertible.

Fig. 1-10. The 1955 Cadillac Eldorado.

Fig. 1-11. In the 1957 Cadillac Eldorado Brougham, Cadillac reached a peak in automobile design.

Cadillacs of 1957 were once again a restyled breed. Lower to the ground, with heavy eyebrows above the headlights and a front end that looks like an altar to the chrome god were the key changes. There is also a gently curving rear deck topped by jutting fins. Power from the dual four-barrel engine is 325. Eldorados of '57, especially the Biarritz, were terrific cars when they were new and they are terrific cars now (Fig. 1-11).

The biggest thing for 1957 though is a car we haven't seen before. It is the all new, $13,050, Eldorado Brougham. It is impossible to imagine anyone looking at this car and thinking Cadillac had run short of elegance.

Here was the most exclusive Cadillac ever produced. Based on the Brougham, Park Avenue and Orleons show cars of the early Fifties, the Eldorado Brougham is a strange and interesting car.

Sitting on a wheelbase of 126 inches, the entire car is 216 inches long, and only 55½ inches high. The 325 horsepower mill sports dual four-barrels and boasts 10:1 compression ratio. The roof is a brushed aluminum affair, just the way Harley Earl liked them. There is air suspension, which is no big thrill for collectors, because the system is so touchy. A total of 45 interior coverings were available to new car buyers in 1957. Inside the glove compartment the new owner found six stainless steel tumblers, mirror and perfume bottle.

But that isn't all. It's got quadruple headlights! In the next two years, this styling touch would become an industry fad (and a long lasting one at that).

There are four doors on the pillarless hardtop and to top it off, they open to the center and lock automatically when closed.

Except for a switch to three-deuce carburetion, and a slight horsepower boost, the 1958 Eldorado Brougham didn't change. The car was in production for only two years, at the end of which, only 704 had been built. Roughly 500 of these are still around for the pleasure of collector's today.

Cadillac's '58 recession line is completely dual headlighted. Like cars from the rest of the industry, they are heavily overchromed. (Remember, restorers, chrome is not the most economical thing to replace when worn.) The Biarritz and the Brougham both have enough good points going for them to overcome any of the bad. Some of the less popular Cadillacs don't fare so well. That's why they're less popular (Fig. 1-12).

It's anybody's guess what happened to Cadillac in 1959. Maybe the boys in design were trying to be funny. Maybe they'd

Fig. 1-12. This 1959 publicity shot tells the whole story of the Fifties all by itself. During the span of time between 1949 and 1960, fins went from small, tasteful bumps to wild, space-age creations.

been sipping too much joy juice. And maybe, they really thought they had found the shape of things to come. Whatever the reason, the Cadillacs of 1959 represent some bizarre styling exercises. Extreme tailfins give the cars a Buck Rogers, space ship look. A rocket-shaped line along the side makes the fins look even more ridiculous. Even Pinin Farina's Eldorado Brougham for 1959-60 is a wild looking, unattractive thing. True, it has the cleanest lines of all the '59's, but it is still very far out.

My pick for the most collectible Cadillac of 1959 is, once again, the Eldorado Biarritz convertible. The engine is a 390 CID, 345 horsepower unit. Suspension is better than in the previous year's model, but these Cadillacs still aren't much when it comes to real handling.

The 1959 Cadillac is a car with which the collector can have a lot of fun. Values will go up, if not quickly, then steadily. Just don't take them or yourself too seriously if you end up owning one.

CHEVROLET

Chevrolets of the Fifties may not be the same high-dollar collectibles the Cadillacs of the decade are, but like their Cadillac cousins, any of the Fifties Chevrolets are collectible. As with the Cadillacs, I will only talk about Chevrolet's most desirable years and models.

Among the great hoards of postwar car collectors, the Chevrolets built from 1950-1959 are far and away the most popular cars in the country. The 1955-57 models hold the same esteemed place with postwar car collectors as the Model A Ford does with collectors of prewar machinery. The most amazing thing is that so many of these mechanical marvels are still seen in this and other countries; many still driven every day. Much sought after '55 - '57 Chevy iron still runs the dirt oval at Hales Corners Speedway in southern Wisconsin.

It was during the Fifties that Chevrolet dropped, for one brief moment in automotive history, to number two in the industry. It was during the Fifties, too, that Chevrolet developed its reputation for building not only durable sedans, but shiny dreamboats and fast-moving sports cars as well.

The 1950 Deluxe Styleline Bel Air is the warm number for that year. There were design elements that would be modified for 1953-54, making those cars second in popularity only to the 1955-57 models (Fig. 1-13). The 1950 Bel Air is fitted with the familiar valve-in-head six. Also mounted (optionally of course) is the not-so-familiar Powerglide, two-speed automatic transmission. CID for that combo is 235, delivering 105 horsepower at 3600 revs. Also in 1950, GM produced its 25 millionth Chevy.

For collectors interested in the first Chevrolets of the decade, it is probably best to consider 1950-52 models as basically the same car. Desirability and values are very close in those years. Engines and transmissions change very little. Styling remains basically the same for all three years with only small changes being noticeable on grille, side moldings and taillights.

Convertibles always have their share of the flair, and are the highest valued 1950-52 Chevs. However, the Bel Air really beats it in looks and is likely to escalate in value a little faster than the rag top now that America's convertible fever has cooled off a bit.

Along with the 1953-54 models, the '50-'51's offer something very valuable to the automotive enthusiast. First, their interiors are like big, comfortable boxes, offering plenty of head, leg and seating room for a family of six, plus a trunk big enough to carry a spare and just about anything else. Second, these cars are powered by very dependable engines, capable of delivering in the neighborhood of 20 miles per gallon. If that isn't a big plus in our fuel-hungry world, nothing is.

Fig. 1-13. The Chevrolet of 1953-54 are often overlooked by enthusiasts searching for '55-57 models. For the time being at least, they are one of the best buys in a Fifties car.

Like all the other GM products, Chevrolets got a big re-style job in 1953. Bodywork was all new, but did not change so drastically as to be unrecognizable from its predecessors. The attention-getting Bel Air became a series unto itself. The lines of the 1953 Chev sharpened and gained definition. A new grille design incorporated three vertical grille bars and round parking lights.

The powerplant for collectors to look for in this one is the new 115 horsepower, 235 cube, hydraulic valve lifted, Blue Flame six, coupled to a Powerglide transmission. One prominent automotive critic has called the Blue Flame the most dependable engine in years and the 1953-54 Chevrolet the most dependable car since the Model A Ford. My own experience tends to confirm that.

In 1954, Chevrolet offered the American public the same basic car it did in 1953. With the kind of car the company was building, there's no fault in that. Again, Bel Air is the top of the line. Again, choose from hardtop, sport coupe and convertible models.

Outward changes for 1954 are minor. The grille grew two new vertical bars, and headlight and taillight rims are revamped. Parking lights are elongated. Bumper guards are turned upside down. Models equipped with powerglide enjoyed a jump of 10 horsepower, up to 125.

Chevrolet for 1953 and 1954, has become pretty popular in its own right during the last few years, but always has taken a back seat to the cars of 1955-57. If you look at current values, you'll discover that this continues to be the case. However, this could change. There are a number of factors at play. First, the styling of the '53 and '54 Chevys, while it flows from the styling of 1949-52, is in a class with the styling of '55-'57. It's clean, it's outstanding for its time, and it's pretty. Very pretty. In fact, there are a lot of enthusiasts who are beginning to think the '53's and '54's are even prettier than the '55-'57's. The Blue Flame six used in '53 and '54 delivers the kind of economical service today's collector needs, even though the Chevys of 1955-57 are pretty efficient little vehicles too. Finally, as the '55-'57's become less and less available, and higher and higher priced, their older siblings start to attract more and more attention.

Keep an eye on these cars. They may easily be part of a coming boom. At present prices, they are right at the top of our "best bets for collectors" list.

In 1955 Chevrolet started a revolution. There is no other way to describe what happened when Chevrolet's 265 CID V-8 hit the streets. The little powerhouse developed by engineer Ed Cole, has become universally recognized as one of the greatest automobile engines ever produced in the entire world. It and its many manifestations set all kinds of records. It became the base for every small block Chevy V-8 to follow. It was economical to produce, easy to work on, and just about the most efficient piece of machinery since the spring-operated mousetrap (Fig. 1-14).

The ohv V-8 of 1955 features a bore and stroke of 3.75 × 3. This first Chevy V-8 since 1919 puts out 170 anxious horses at roughly 4,400 revs with Powerglide. It weighs less than the old Blue Flame. With the dual exhaust and four-barrel Power Pac, horsepower is upped to 180. Obviously, Chevrolet was making one hell of an entry into the postwar performance race. This entry didn't go unnoticed by contemporary enthusiasts either.

For high speed, point-A-to-point-B driving, '55's were available with stick overdrive. This is the hot combo for collectors, though Powerglide is quite popular with the less powerful engines.

In 1955, a Chevrolet was GM's 50 millionth car built. As if bringing out one of the finest engines ever wasn't enough, Chevy also got some of the best styling of the decade.

At first glance, the '55 Chevy is just one box on top of another. On further inspection, first impressions become modified considerably. Every line is well defined. The rear window line is the same attractive design as the Corvette hardtop. There is a

Fig. 1-14. A pristine example, like this one, of a 1955 Chevy Bel Air convertible will cost you, but it's probably worth it.

pronounced dimple at the beltline and a wraparound windshield. The grille is an egg crate based on one Ferrari had used.

In 1955 Chevs, pick either the Bel Air hardtop, sport coupe or convertible. Here you get the new body at its best, a little extra chrome and some terrific looking, original, two tone paint jobs. Other Chevs of the year are plentiful but they aren't worth near as much in enthusiast circles.

Except, that is, for the prettiest station wagon you ever saw, the Chevrolet Bel Air Nomad (Fig. 1-15). The Nomad is the bastard son of two body styles that happen to go together smartly. Take a Chevy station wagon, breed it with a two-door hardtop and the Nomad is born. Now, just for the sake of good looks, throw in a wraparound rear window and seven vertical chrome strips on the tailgate (Fig. 1-16). What you end up with is a certified milestone with plenty of wow, worth over $10,000 in perfect condition (Fig. 1-17).

Among enthusiasts, the battle has raged for years on whether the 1955 or 1957 model is the best-looking mid-Fifties Chevy. Everyone has his own opinion, but one thing is clear. In almost every one of these arguments, no mention is made of the spectacular 1956 models. These babies are my favorites (Fig. 1-18).

The 1956 Chevy is a modification of the '55. But even small changes, when done correctly, can make a difference. The '56's

Fig. 1-15. Just about the most popular station wagon ever produced, the Chevy Nomad. This is the 1955 version.

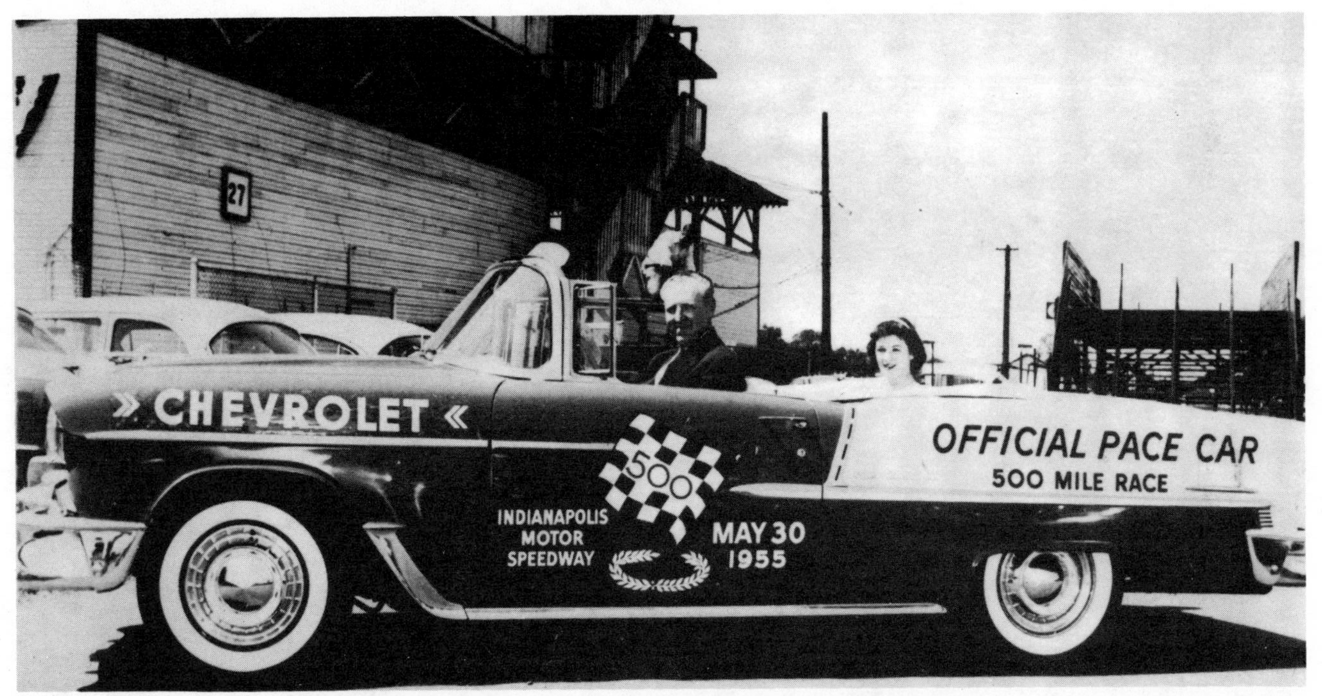

Fig. 1-16. On May 30, 1955, a Bel Air convertible led the pack around the track at Indy. A pace car replica will always be worth a couple grand more than its undecorated kin.

Fig. 1-17. Here's a strictly stock version of the 1956 Chevy Nomad.

Fig. 1-18. Notice the mag wheels. Mid century Chevs are popular with hop-up boys as well as the restorers.

have a sweeping look, accentuated by the chrome trim running all the way to the front of the car and back to the point where the rear wheel well begins, then curving down to the rear bumper. The wheel wells themselves follow approximately the same trajectory.

Front wheel wells on the '56 are slightly more rounded. The front grille has widened to include the parking lights and combined with the bumper to create a mass of chrome. The effect is less attractive, but more interesting and indicative of the decade than the '55 (Fig. 1-19).

The rear fenders don't carry fins. Their shape, however, is just suggestive enough to be good looking. The Nomad was back again, with the same basic styling changes as the rest of the Bel Air line.

If you're a collector looking for a bargain in mid-Fifty Bel Airs, 1956 is where you will find it. Prices are high, but somewhat less than for 1955 and 1957 models. Buy now—they're bound to catch up.

The 1957 Chevrolet Bel Airs are a definite concession to the chromed and finny god. The bumper/grille has become a mass of bright-work divided by a long horizontal bar of the same stuff. Twin chrome ornaments shoot out of rises at the extreme front of the hood. Headlight shrouds are chromed and pronounced. Just behind the headlights, on the side of each fender, is a group of three chrome notches. A strip of chrome that begins at the headlight

THE
CHEVRO
CHEVROLET
You're looking at a real, honest-to-goodness beauty queen—and you've got to admit the looking's good. The '56 Chevrolet stretches low and clean from its big new grille to those rakish, high-set taillights. There's bold distinction in that sweeping speedline chrome treatment. Every detail, outside and in, reflects the car's colorful good taste.
Naturally, there's new power to go with those new looks. Horsepower ratings that range up to 205 for shot-like acceleration and safer passing. But, more importantly, this is a great road car. It proved it on Pikes Peak, streaking up that snaky ribbon of a road to set a new record. Chevrolet beat the mountain and showed that safety is *built into* a car with things like sports-car cornering, precise steering, solid roadability and ruggedness.
Yes sir, show car *and* road car, the '56 Chevrolet is a winner in either league. We think you'll have a lot of fun proving this to yourself.
SEE YOUR CHEVROLET DEALER
Bel Air

Fig. 1-19. In '56, Chevy said, "The hot one's even hotter." And they weren't lyin'.

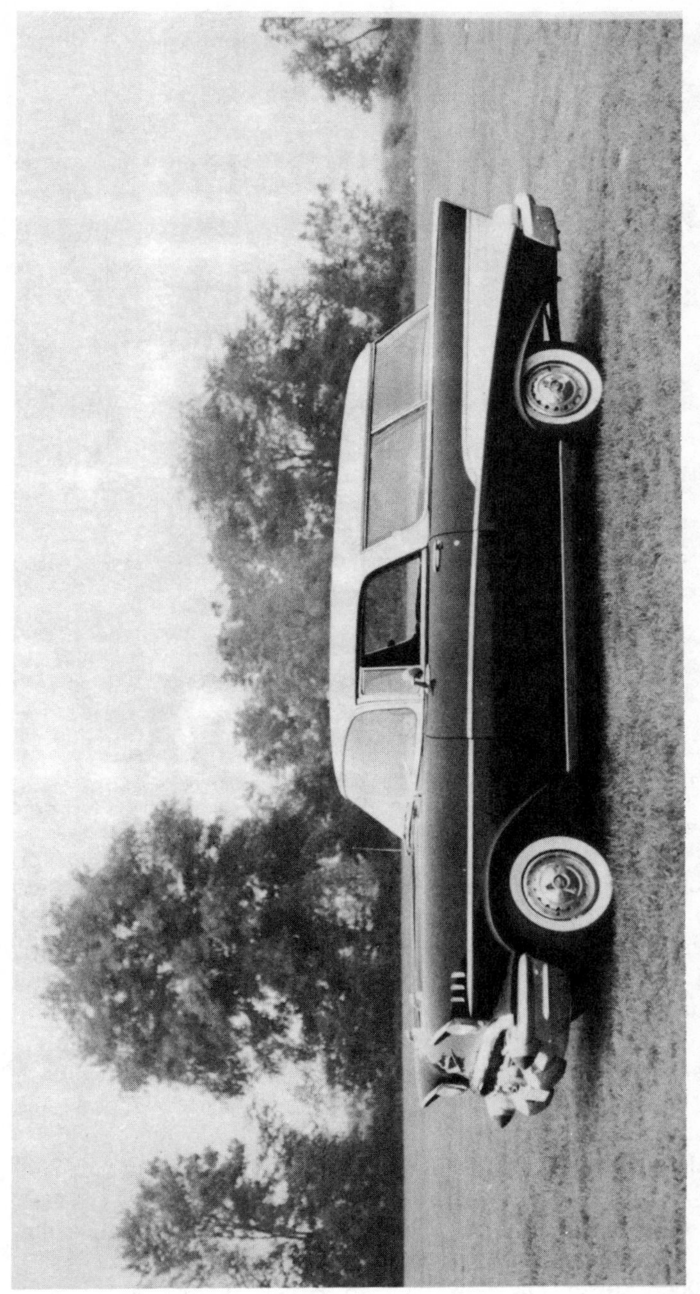

Fig. 1-20. A 1957 Chevrolet Nomad sport wagon.

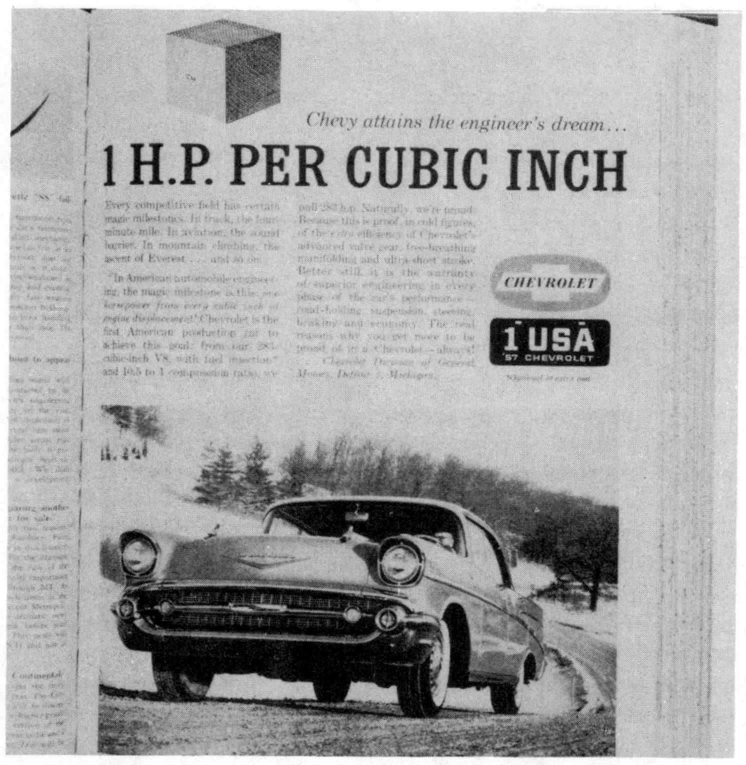
Chevy attains the engineer's dream...
1 H.P. PER CUBIC INCH
CHEVROLET
1 USA
'57 CHEVROLET

Fig. 1-21. In 1957, Chevy got a new 283 with fuel injection optional. The result? One horsepower per one cubic inch. (Well, there were actually a few extra horses, but Chevy big shots liked the one-for-one idea.)

shroud, shoots back to just beyond the belt line dip and separates into two widely separated chrome strips, between which is cleverly placed more chrome and color. At the very rear, you will find two of the smallest, most useless taillights in automotive history.

This, my friends, is the most popular Chev of the Fifties. Wheel size was reduced from 15 to 14 inches, resulting in a lower car. Wheelbase stayed at the same 115 inches as 1956, but overall length grew to 200 inches. The suspension lost a lot of its tightness from the previous two years and handling is a lot better (Fig. 1-20).

The big news for 1957 is under the hood. In 1955, Chevy became "the hot one." In 1957, those words got new meaning. First, the nifty little 265 cuber has become a 283 (Fig. 1-21). Second, Power Pac now includes a pair of four-barrel pots.

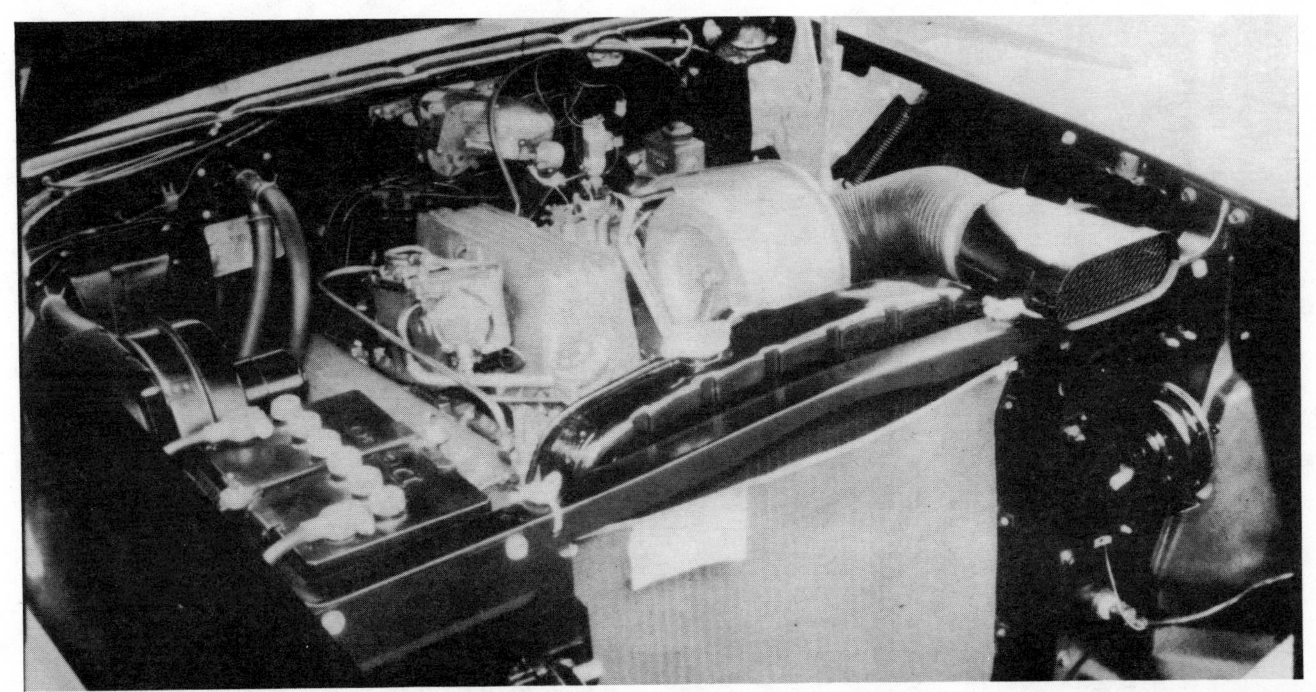

Fig. 1-22. The absolute hottest setup you could lay your hands on in a '57 Chevrolet. This fine example shows the standard fuel injection setup with a super-rare air intake scoop (from NASCAR Chevs) added.

Third—this is the biggie—a brand new fuel injection unit mounted on that 283 makes it the first engine in the industry to develop one horsepower for each and every cubic inch. This sounds impressive enough now. Think what it meant in 1957. To be specific, it meant you could shoot down the highway faster than just about anybody, mounted on one of the most noticeable steeds ever to come out of Detroit (Fig. 1-21).

When 1958 rolled around, America got an all new Chevrolet. The top of the line Bel Air was topped by an addition known as the Impala in sport coupe and convertible styles (Fig. 1-23).

The new Chevies had taken on rounded, softer lines. They were also longer (117-inch wheel base), lower to the ground and wider than the hybrids before them. The best thing you can say about the shape of '58 is that it still doesn't have the fins that soared up everywhere else in the industry.

The '58's grille is a wide mesh affair with twin parking lights popping out of it. Headlights are doubled, too. Perched atop each of the front fenders are styled chrome ornaments. There are now four chrome notches on the front fender. A big chrome whatzit, looking something like a backward mounted air scoop fills the space between chrome strip and rocker panel, door and wheel well. As much as any car produced in the Fifties, the Chevies of 1958 are big, crowd-stopping dreamboats.

The small block 283 is capable of 230 horsepower with a four-barrel carb, or 250 with fuel injection. A brand new, big block, 348 CID V-8 puts out a base 250 horses or 280 when mounted with three deuces.

These cars hadn't been especially popular with collectors until recently, so prices are still fairly low, as is demand (Fig. 1-24).

In model year 1959, Chevrolet gave in to the fin. Let me tell you, when Chevy gave in, they gave in big. While nearly everybody else's fins were shooting off into the skys, Chevy's went out instead of up. They are incredible; while the '59 Chevs are a little bizarre, they are also attractive. The rear end of this thing is real space age stuff with cat's eye taillights to enhance the affect (Fig. 1-25).

Impala became a model all its own. The Impala, and all 1959 Chevies, sat on a 119-inch wheelbase. These cars had grown a lot since the decade began. During the Fifties, big was beautiful. By that standard, the 1959 Chev made it. The flat roof and wraparound rear window of the hardtop Impala help to make its look second only to the Impala convertible.

Fig. 1-23. One of the better buys in a Fifties Chev, the 1958 Impala.

OLDSMOBILE

The Oldsmobile branch of GM is every bit as outstanding in the Fifties as the rest of the GM gang with a fair share of firsts. Styling gets a big A+. When you have a Fifties Olds, you have one dependable automobile. Yet except for a very few models, Oldsmobiles fill an extremely small part of the vast numbers of collector cars. When we apply our working definitions of dreamboats and milestones as the hottest collector cars, even fewer Oldsmobiles fit.

Fig. 1-24. Factory continental kits like the one on this 1959 Chevy Impala are rare and desirable options.

Among the really hot collectible Oldsmobiles, we can start with the De Luxe Holiday hardtop and convertible (Fig. 1-26). These cars have a body in common with the Chevrolet Bel Air of the same vintage. They were made available in incarnations of 119.5 inches and 122 inches. The De Luxe Holiday convertible was available only with the 122 inch wheelbase. In other words, there are three choices among the cream to choose from. All fall into the Futuramic line.

The hot engine to have in your 1950 Olds is the 303 CID Rocket 88 V-8. This landmark motor puts out some 135 stampeding horses, that will take it from stoplight to 60 mph in a rushing 12 seconds. Mounted with Olds' proven Hydra-Matic, the Rocket is good for a top end in the 100 mph neighborhood. The Rocket emblem, with the flying 88 across it is a Fifties car collector's status symbol (Fig. 1-27).

The Rocket engine was originally intended for use only on the big Olds 98, but somebody decided it might make for a nifty mill in the 88. The results speak for themselves. The Rockets became the first big NASCAR winners of the decade. They also won the Mexican Road Race of 1950 and set some sand scorching records at Daytona as well (Fig. 1-28).

The next zinger to enter the Olds line came in 1953, a year that previous pages have already established as a milestone. In the same class as the 1953 Buick Skylark and Cadillac Eldorado, is the 1953 Oldsmobile 98 Fiesta convertible coupe (Fig. 1-29). Like Skylark and Eldorado, Fiesta arrived on the scene as an expensive—$6,000—limited edition—458 copies—production custom job.

The Fiesta's 303 cube Rocket produces 170 horses. It is cranked over by a 12-volt electrical system. Along the standard

Fig. 1-25. Take a look at two of the greatest fins of the Fifties; circa 1959.

Fig. 1-26. The Olds 88 in Holiday coupe form. The Rocket engine is big, powerful and reliable. What a combination.

power features are the good old Hydra-Matic, power brakes, steering, windows and seats.

Besides the same cut down, wraparound windshield as Eldo and Skylark, there is a custom leather interior, spinner wheel covers and nifty two tone paint schemes. The Fiesta doesn't have the same hulking animal look as the special edition Buicks and Cads; instead, it looks like a youthful, happy-go-lucky, lickety-split machine.

I think it ranks a cut above its contemporaries, even the other special editions. A value that is very close to $20,000 seems to suggest that other enthusiasts feel the same.

Oldsmobiles of 1954 got a complete restyling job. The resulting body style remained through model year 1956. Available wheelbases were 122-inch 88's and 126-inch 98's. The basic V-8 for those years is a 324 cuber. The Oldsmobile styling included the Fiesta's panoramic windshield and other Fiesta touches.

In 1955, Oldsmobile built a record 583,180 cars. The year's big facelift was accompanied by a major nose job. The shape stayed the same as '54, but was updated by the use of a new grille, recessed headlights and an optional glass boot for convertible tops. There were also new two-tone color combinations.

The most desirable '55 Olds with today's collectors is the Classic 98 convertible. The car sits on a 126-inch wheelbase and is best powered by the 202 horse Rocket. The Super 88's of the same vintage are similar in appearance, but mounted on a shorter wheelbase. If you can't lay hands on the 98, the 88 will easily do.

In 1956, the new Olds Starfire convertible was introduced. The front end was restyled to include a massive grille that looks like the mouth of a large chrome bass with a wide chrome post holding its lips apart. The 324 cube mill in the Starfire puts out 240 horsepower with a four-barrel accompanied by Hydra-Matic drive; now known as Jetaway Hydra-Matic.

The '56 Olds Starfire convertible was originally priced at just under $3,700. Some 8,581 of them were produced. At a current value of roughly $8,000, about 50 to 100 are said to still exist.

The last Oldsmobile we'll consider in our list of dreamboats and milestones came along in 1957 as part of the all-new, restyled Olds line. The car is the top-of-the-line Olds 98 Starfire coupe and convertible. The lines of the '57 Olds are clean and elegant. The slightly reshaped fish mouth grille continues.

These cars are real dreamboats; more modern than their predecessors, much more attractive than their immediate juniors.

The big plus for the '57 is the famous J-2 Rocket engine, an $83 option when new, but worth considerably more to collectors today. The J-2 Rocket's 371 cubes produce 300 horsepower, with three dueces mounted for carburetion.

PONTIAC

With Pontiac, as with Oldsmobile, there is plenty for the collector to choose from in a wide variety of prices. During the Fifties Pontiac built some sturdy cars, some pretty cars and, like many other car companies, some garish cars. But very few of them fit into the dreamboat or milestone niche.

Only the 1955-57 Safaris are certified milestones (Fig. 1-30). Only the far out, overdecorated 1958 Bonneville convertible was an Indy Pace Car. Other than that, a small portion of Pontiac's

Fig. 1-27. Oldsmobile ad men called the 88 "the big number with the new low price for 1950."

Fig. 1-28. 1950 Series 88 Oldsmobile Deluxe Holiday coupe.

1950-59 production had the combination of glitter, go power and indescribable eye appeal that made them the special kind of cars that were dreamboats when they hit the showroom floor and are still considered as such today (Fig. 1-31).

The peak of the early Fifties for Pontiac came in 1953 in the Chieftain Deluxe and Custom Catalina lines. The '53 Pontiacs are similar to the Pontiacs that preceded them. They are, however, larger cars than their predecessors. The windshield consists of only one piece; the grille and bumper arrangement cover less of the front and takes on a Fifties look as opposed to the Forties look of previous model years. Probably most indicative of their place in history, the 1953 Pontiacs produced a bump on the rear fender that

Fig. 1-29. The 1953 Oldsmobile Fiesta. If you own one of these my friend, you own a gold mine.

Fig. 1-30. Pontiac's 1955 answer to the Chevrolet Nomad. It was, I might add, the right answer. Call it Safari.

can't be mistaken for anything but—you guessed it—a fin. Cadillac influence is obvious here.

Hydra-Matic became, in 1953, an extremely popular option. (Because of a factory fire midway through 1953, some 18,000 Pontiacs of '53 and '54 vintage are fitted with Powerglide transmissions produced by Chevrolet.) Power steering became an option. Wheelbase is 122 inches. The best engine available in 1953 was still the old in-line, L-head, 268 cube eight.

The 1954 Pontiacs are not a very exciting re-make of the '53's. For my money, 1954 is best remembered as the year Pontiac should have restyled, but didn't.

Instead, the big change came for Pontiacs in 1955. I'll get to styling changes in a minute. But first, the best news: Pontiac got the overhead valve V-8 everyone was expecting in '54. The Strato Streak (hot damn!), as Pontiac decided to call the new engine, is 287 cubes, with base horsepower at 180. With the optional four-barrel, you get 200 of the four-legged little devils. Compression is 8:1. If you haven't already guessed, that's more than enough to make the old chief shake his tail.

Beyond the powerplant, there is a panoramic windshield, bigger bumps at the end of the rear fenders, 12-volt electrical system and tubeless tires. Terrific two-tone color combinations abound.

For Pontiac's standard series 1955 models, the Star Chief convertible and Custom Star Chief Catalinas are hot stuff. If you want a dreamboat, pick one of these.

If, on the other hand, you're milestone shopping, consider Pontiac's version of the Chevy Nomad. It's called the Star Chief Custom Safari. Again, hardtop and wagon give birth to one nifty machine. While the Safari doesn't have the same super clean line of the Nomad, it does follow the same basic format; wide center pillar, wraparound rear window and all. Besides that, with Safari you get two-tone coverage and, of course, the little Pontiac bump—chrome edged—on the rear fenders.

In 1956, changes were minor. The models from that year look much like the '55's, but they just don't have quite the pizazz of the '55. That is, of course, until you take a look at the mechanical end of things.

For 1956, the Strato Streak engine added some performance weight. Still basically the same V-8, it now delivers 227 horsepower from its 316 cubes when mounted with a four-barrel carb. Now that doesn't exactly put it in the same performance class as Chevy's far out and fantastic little 265 of the same vintage, but it isn't a slug either.

The Safari? Like the Nomad, it had two more good years ('56 and '57) left in it. And, like the Nomad, all three years bring a premium in the collector car market today.

The Pontiacs of 1957 arrived on the scene in new skin (Fig. 1-32). There is an obvious flow in styling from the 1955-56 models, but they are a good deal more than just facelifts. While the cars are actually a bit smaller than their predecessors, sleeker styling gives them a longer look by comparison. Contributing to this look is a long trim panel that runs from front fender to rear. The little fin-like bump that graces the rear fender of other Fifties Pontiacs is

Fig. 1-31. In 1957, Pontiac's Safari "landed the prize." A little garish compared to 1955, but still much sought after.

Fig. 1-32. The fabulous 1957 Bonneville by Pontiac, with fuel injection.

gone. Instead there is a sharp, well defined fender line that cuts back into the car just above the taillight in a not unfinlike appearance of its own. In silhouette, the '57 Pontiac bears distinct resemblance to the '57 Chevy. Also, like the '57 Chevy, a switch was made from 15-to 14-inch wheels.

Grille and bumper are heavier. Two tone paint jobs are a little more stylish. On the most desirable '57 Pontiac of all, the Star Chief Bonneville, there's a row of seven brief chrome notches decorating the front fender behind the wheelwell. All of the '57 Pontiacs were given the new 347 CID V-8. That's pretty impressive by itself; now add fuel injection, a racing cam and hydraulic lifters and you have excitement plus. Today, the 1957 Pontiac Bonneville with fuel injection is one of the most sought after and valuable cars of the decade. If you didn't want fuel injection back then, there was a tri-power setup that's capable of delivering nearly as much performance. Recently, a friend offered me a blank check if I could successfully act as a middleman between him and a perfect California example of one of these fine machines.

Recession year styling of 1958 made the Pontiacs of that year truly overdone, super gaudy, Fifties dreamboats (Fig. 1-33). Lots of chrome, lots of color and styling, all of which makes these cars look like they're taking off even when they're standing still.

Bodies are about the same size, just a hair longer and wider than the '57's. They are lower though; noticeably so. The side-trim panel is fatter. The bumper and grille area, believe it or not, are less ostentatious than in 1957. Vertical chrome notches behind the wheel well on the front fender are replaced by four much larger pieces of horizontal chrome trim.

Fig. 1-33. A "bold new Bonneville" from Pontiac for 1958.

All Hydra-Matic equipped Pontiacs were eligible for fuel injected or tri carb Tempest V-8's. The engine is made up of 370 cubes and capable of up to 310 horsepower depending on which engine option is mounted.

By virtue of becoming a model of its own and being chosen to pace the 1958 Indianapolis 500, my pick for collectors is the 1958 Bonneville, especially in convertible form (Fig. 1-34). But don't look down your nose at the Bonneville sport coupe either. Both are neat, sporty and guaranteed to escalate in both value and desirability.

Fig. 1-34. In 1958, a Pontiac paced at Indy with 1957 winner Sam Hanks at the wheel. That's Tony Hulman standing.

Fig. 1-35A. The 1959 Pontiac Bonneville looking for everything like the king of the road.

The year 1959 is a true milestone in Pontiac history; even though no '59 Pontiac is yet certified as a milestone by the Milestone Car Society. This was the year Pontiac divided its grille in half and went off wide trackin'. This also is the year Pontiac outdid everyone else in the fin game. Oh, Pontiac's fins weren't the largest, they weren't the chromiest, and they weren't the most grotesque. In fact, I think they are quite attractive. What makes the 1959 Pontiac fins so special is that each rear fender has *two*.

Fig. 1-35B. From this angle—in fact, from most angles—the '59 Pontiac looks a mile long.

All things considered, the '59 Pontiacs are pretty nice looking automobiles. My pick for the best of the bunch is the Bonneville, primarily the convertible. Here some 4000 pounds of iron is distributed neatly over a 124-inch wheelbase (Figs. 1-35A & B).

To finish it off, the '59 Pontiac's mill is a big 389 cube affair. With the optional three double-barrel carbs added, you get a super duper 315 of the finest Indian ponies in the Fifties horsepower race. Bonneville, Catalina and Star Chief are the final Fifties model names. By 1959, Chieftain and Super Chief are just a vague memory.

Chapter 2 Ford Motor Company

During the Fifties, the three FoMoCo lines—Ford, Lincoln, Mercury— produced some interesting cars, some powerful cars, some exciting cars and some outstanding cars. To many enthusiasts and collectors, Ford automobiles of the fab Fifties are among the most attractive FoMoCo products ever produced. Yet, where Ford products make up better than half of the pre-WWII car hobby, they play a decided second fiddle to General Motors machines in the postwar hobby; especially the Fifties portion of it. With a few exceptions, like the Mark II Lincoln Continental and the first Thunderbirds (Thunderbirds are treated in a separate chapter with Corvettes), Ford products just don't get collected like General Motor products do.

It doesn't take an especially well-trained eye, however, to look at the Ford lines of the Fifties and see that some exceptional cars were produced. You don't even have to include the Edsel. In fact, I won't be including the Edsel. A great number of the dreamboats of the Fifties were and are considered such because of their outlandish styles, wild fins and crazy paint schemes. But somehow these cars developed a strength of character all their own. They are noticed first for their outstanding physical appearance, but usually are accepted as collectable for attributes other than whatever questionable physical appeal they have.

Edsels do not fit into that group. Edsels are more or less cult cars. They are great fun, and so are the people who own them, but they just simply don't fit the criteria that makes an automobile either a dreamboat or a milestone.

Take heart. As I said earlier, the Ford Motor Company built a lot of nifty Fifties cars (Fig. 2-1).

FORD

There's no problem at all picking the first hot collectable Fords of the decade. Just a glance at the whole model line-up will have the Crestliner and the Custom Deluxe convertible practically leaping out at you.

The specially trimmed Crestliner was Ford's attempt to provide a sporty car with sedan-sized accommodations. The price for the 1950 model was $1,711; the '51 cost, $1,595. It is, upon examination, a dressed up two-door featuring sweeping side trim and a two-tone paint job in the form of a contrast panel (Fig. 2-2). Also available on Crestliner was the first vinyl roof for steel-topped automobiles, including an eye catching houndstooth version. These cars don't exist in great numbers today, but every once in a while one turns up for sale making them well worth looking for.

The other choice 1950-51 Ford would be the Custom DeLuxe convertible. For power in the Crestliner or convertible, look for the 239 cube flat-head V-8 with stick in 1950 and Fordomatic two-speed in '51.

Ford styling in the opening years of the Fifties is entirely different from that of Chevy, especially in '50 and '51, but equally as clean and attractive. Already in 1950, Ford had taken on the

Fig. 2-1. Ford's convertible for 1950.

squared style lines that characterize the cars of the 50's while Chevy was still working, successfully, with the rounded lines of the Forties.

For 1952, Fords were completely restyled. That restyling was so well thought out, so successful, that it formed the basis for Ford design through 1956. The head of design for Ford at the time was George Walker whose design made the 1952 Ford the first car to be radically changed to meet the mood of the decade.

The body of the 1952 Ford had more shape than Fords immediately before it. The rear fender is prime for a fender fin, though they didn't actually show up until 1957, only being hinted at in 1955 and '56. A bump along the rear quarter panel gives the look of a long fender skirt begun in front of the wheel well with a fairly large, vertical piece of chrome.

The windshield on the '52 is one piece and slightly curved; rear window glass has even more of a curve to it than the front. The grille is a good looking arrangement with three of Ford's well-known, decorative spinners.

The 1952 Crestline, in Victoria and convertible clothing, is the first choice among enthusiasts. Both cars sit on a 115-inch wheelbase and can be had with V-8 power and Fordomatic tranny. (For performance though, don't overlook the overhead valve six with stick and overdrive. The flat-head can be dressed up with plenty of aftermarket performance options, but the six was just about as fast in stock form.)

In 1953, a Ford Crestline convertible was chosen to lead the pack around the track at Indy on Memorial Day (Fig. 2-3). This car is valued highly enough among enthusiasts and collectors in its plainest form, but one of the Pace Car replicas will be worth half again as much.

What else makes the '53 Ford special? First, 1953 was Ford's big golden anniversary year, though no especially large amount of hoopla attended the occasion. Second, this was the last year for the outdated flathead.

Also in 1953, power steering became an option for the first time on a Ford. Visually, the '53 is almost identical to the '52. Taillights are slightly different. The front grille is modified to connect with the bumper (visually) and triple spinners are replaced by one flat, bullet shaped ornament. A spear of chrome cuts through the rear quarter bubble (Fig. 2-4).

The Fords of 1954 give their makers plenty to brag about. They mark the beginning of a new era, with the introduction of an

Fig. 2-2. In 1950, Ford didn't have a hardtop, but what they did have was a special, trim-optioned Crestliner, with a two-tone paint job and vinyl roof.

overhead valve, Y-block V-8 and cubic inches numbering 239 released 130 horses. The new engine is much quieter and more powerful than the old flatheads. A heartier front suspension combines with the motor to make this the best performing Ford so far.

Styling on the '54 Ford is basically the same as '52 and '53, with revised grille and other chrome. There is, however, one very big addition to the line in terms of style: the new Crestline Skyliner hardtop.

The most notable difference in this new Ford is the tinted plexiglass roof insert. An accompanying headliner can be snapped into place to keep out the sun or anything else that peeks in from above. When not in use, the headliner may be rolled up and stashed in a pouch near the glove compartment. The Skyliner was intended to be an attention getter to draw people into Ford showrooms. I can't say whether the plan worked or not. I can say, though, that Ford Skyliners attract attention every place they show up nowadays.

Over 13,000 Skyliners were produced in 1954 at a price of $2,241. Some 100 or so of them are probably still around today.

In 1955, Ford began a two-year run of its most attractive standard passenger cars of the Fifties. During that milestone year, most companies engaged in a major restyle. Ford didn't. What Ford did do was perform some real, honest to goodness automotive

Fig. 2-3. A fine '53 Ford including Continental kit. Its good looks can't be faulted, even next to GM's spectacular 1953 offerings.

Fig. 2-4. Ford's special edition pace car for the 1953 Indy 500. Get a load of those nifty wire wheels.

magic on the design thay had been using since 1952. The result? Talk about two-toned and chromed pretty babies; the '55 Fords were right on the money. Still are. While slightly more chrome covered, the design of the '55 Ford is every bit as clean and attractive as the '55 Chev.

Here's a glance at some of the things that Frank Hershey, the man at the lead in '55 styling, did to update the three-year-old look. Bumper/grille arrangement got a modern touch, similar to that of the '55 Thunderbird, with protruding bullet shaped parking lamps. Just above that are heavily hooded headlights, also resembling the little sporting car. A front-to-back chrome strip is a sweeping piece of work that adds to the car's rakish look. The windshield has a much truer curve to it. Rear fenders are sharper, hinting at the fins that arrived in 1957. The fender-skirt-like bubble on the lower rear quarter (smaller than'54) is echoed on the lower front quarter.

The best looking Ford of the Fifties is the 1955 Ford Fairlane Crown Victoria (Fig. 2-5). It has all of the above plus a tiara like chrome band that goes from the door post area up and over the top of the car. And the best part is that some of these dreamboats were built with the Skyliner option. Neat! Base price for the new Crown Vic was $2,302; the Skyliner's tinted see-through top added $70 to that. These cars still fall a bit behind the Chevs of the same year in enthusiast desirability and collector value, so they can be had now for a few dollars less.

Ford became one of the leaders in the performance race when the overhead valve V-8 was added in 1954. For 1955, the base V-8 delivered 162 horses from 272 cubes. A performance-minded buyer could have the Thunderbird V-8 which put out 182 horsepower with 8.5:1 compression ratio, four-barrel carburetor and dual exhausts. All '55 Fords sit on a 115.5-inch wheelbase.

In 1956, styling stayed about the same as the previous year. Visually, grille and parking lights are updated. Chrome side trim is much the same, but wider.

Safety became very important in 1956 and was available in standard equipment and option form. Put all together, you could have a padded dash, padded sun visors, dished steering wheel, factory installed seat belts, better brakes and a special rear view mirror. All of these things piled up in Ford ad copy. There is some question, though, whether or not all the safety add-ons had any effect in adding new Ford buyers. What probably did matter was the availabilty of the 292 CID, 202 horsepower Thunderbird engine in all Ford models.

Fig. 2-5. Ford introduced the Crown Victoria in 1955. Almost since that day, it has held a special place in the hearts of Ford lovers the world over. With the special (optional) plexiglass top, they are neat.

1. The magic begins when you touch the button marked "Top". .

3. And then the top separates from the body . . .

5. Lower and lower sinks the top. Front piece tucks under . . .

2. Smoothly, electric motors lift the rear deck lid . . .

4. Up and back goes the top. Front piece folds down . . .

6. Now the rear deck lid starts to lower itself . . .

Fig. 2-6. The 1957 Ford Skyliner, "birth of a mechanical miracle." The miracle is that they work almost as good as Ford claimed they would.

During the rest of the decade Ford restyled again and again in an attempt to capture some of the excitement going on elsewhere in the automotive look of the Fifties. Ford's new look included fins and the newer, bigger engines. But the fact is, Ford's final three Fifties model years were boring. Dull, dull, dull, with one exception: the 1957 Ford Fairlane 500 Skyliner retractable hardtop (Fig. 2-6). The old Skyliner's let you take a peek at the sky above. This one gives you the whole show, just like any other convertible.

The complicated retractable top with its many motors, circuits, circuit breakers and relays cost customers about $300 more than the standard convertible. The Skyliner is some three inches longer than the base Fairlane and the roof is equally shorter. The top retracts automatically into the luggage compartment with trunk lid popping itself open backward (Fig. 2-7).

From the birth of retractable production in 1957 to the end in 1959, roughly 50,000 models were produced. They are the only Fifties Fords, beside the Thunderbirds of 1955-57, certified as milestones by the Milestone Car society.

LINCOLN

Looking at Lincoln in the Fifties, we discover three Capris that are certified milestones; one that should be; and two years of a milestone Continental.

Two similar, basic body styles were used to produce the full-fledged dreamboat Continentals and the fine performance Capris. Both are legends that will draw a crowd wherever lovers of the automotive art gather. For those of you who may not know, the Lincoln Capris were built by Lincoln/Mercury Division of Ford Motor Company and Continentals were produced by a separate Continental Division. The reason I'm treating both together here is that in the hobby the two are generally considered in the same breath.

The 1950-51 Lincolns were nothing more than big, ugly Mercuries. Oh, these big Lincolns had plenty going for them, but their bumpy bathtub shapes just couldn't sell the buying public in big numbers. If Lincoln was going to compete, especially in Cadillac's price range, then something had to be done.

In 1952, Lincoln emerged as a good looking, cleanly styled super car: high on style, capable of becoming king of the Carrera Panamericana (better known as the Mexican Road Race). They are big. They are pretty. They are fast. They hold the road like bubble gum. From the whole crop, the hottest numbers then and now are the Capri and Capri convertible.

The Lincoln Capris are from one year to the next, very much the same machine, so we can take a look at the group together here.

The '52-'54 Lincolns graced a 123-inch wheelbase; a little shorter than one might expect. Their look is much like that of the Fords of the same period, but slightly stretched for a more streamlined look. Interior room is also better than Ford. Interior quality is high, full of the finest fabrics and workmanship.

Of course there is a great deal more to a car than the shape of the body and the cut of the carpets. The 1952-54 models were factory-fitted with Lincoln's new 317 CID, 160 horsepower (205 in '53-'54), valve in head V-8. While not generally considered as such, this is a milestone engine, overshadowed, (as was everything at the time), only by Chevy's magnificent little small-block, overhead valve V-8. Maybe I am being too generous about the Lincoln mill, but I can say without hesitation that this unit far exceeds the one it replaces.

It isn't a big secret that the Mexican Road Race Lincolns weren't exactly the same cars that could be bought off the showroom floor. Those flying machines were beefed up with truck cams, mechanical lifters, special wheels and spindles, higher rear axle ratio and export suspension. However, the magic is transferable. Besides, if you can get one of these '52-'54 Lincolns in hardtop form, you can always put in some research time and restore/

Fig. 2-7. This 1958 Ford retractable shows the proper way to display one at car shows; or in your driveway if you're selling it.

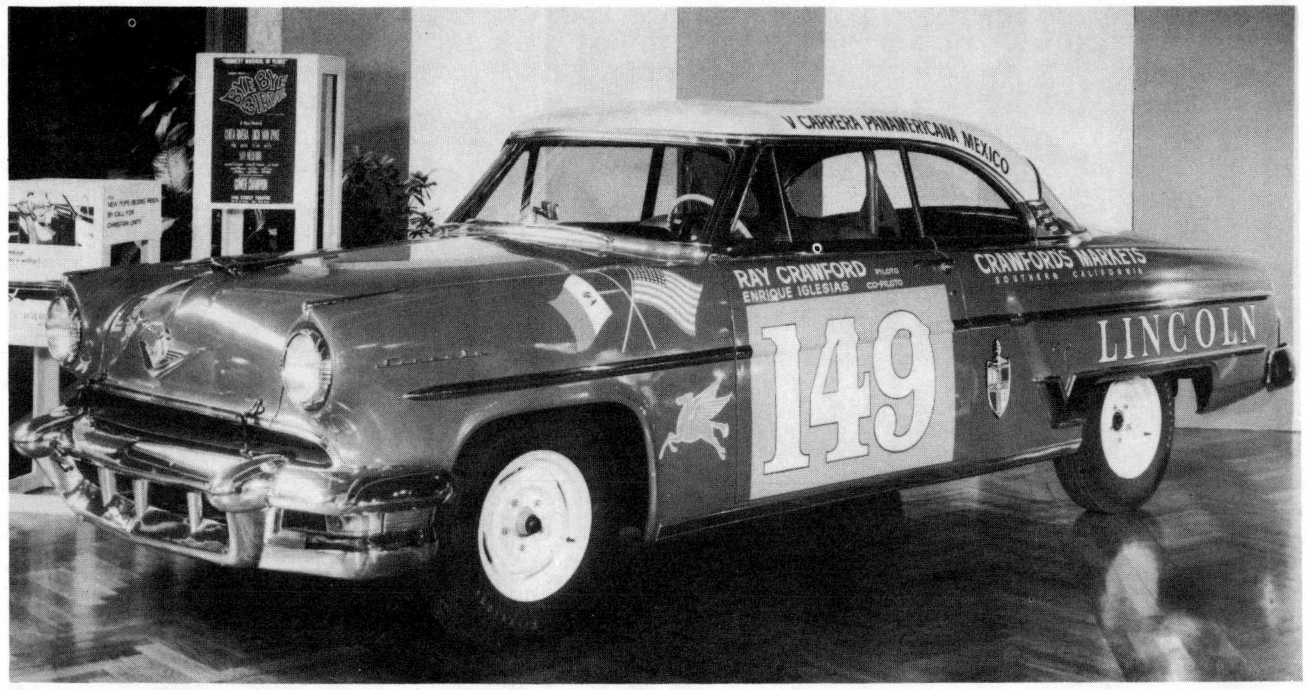

Fig. 2-8. A legend in road racing, the 1953 Lincoln Capri. This mother made the Carrera Panamericana Mexico—better known as the Mexican Road Race—look like a Sunday drive.

rebuild it as a Mexican Road Race replica. By the way, Lincoln took the top slots in the Carrera Panamericana in all three years (Fig. 2-8).

For luxury in these cars, look for power steering, power seats, air conditioning and noise insulation. For a luxury ride with performance plus, consider the '52-'54 Lincolns. If you want a little extra flash, get yourself the rag top version (Fig. 2-9).

The 1955 Lincoln Capris retained the same body shell, with some small styling changes. Instead of going to the more fully wraparound windshield that was becoming popular with the other manufacturers, Lincoln stuck with the old standby. The car doesn't look any worse for it either. Overall weight went up about 100 pounds while wheelbase stayed the same. Chromework is slightly heavier, but not overdone (Fig. 2-10).

Turbo Drive became Lincoln's very own automatic tranny in 1955. The V-8 powerplant sports dual exhausts and is 341

Fig. 2-9. In 1954, Lincoln ads played on the car's big racing wins in introducing the restyled '54 models.

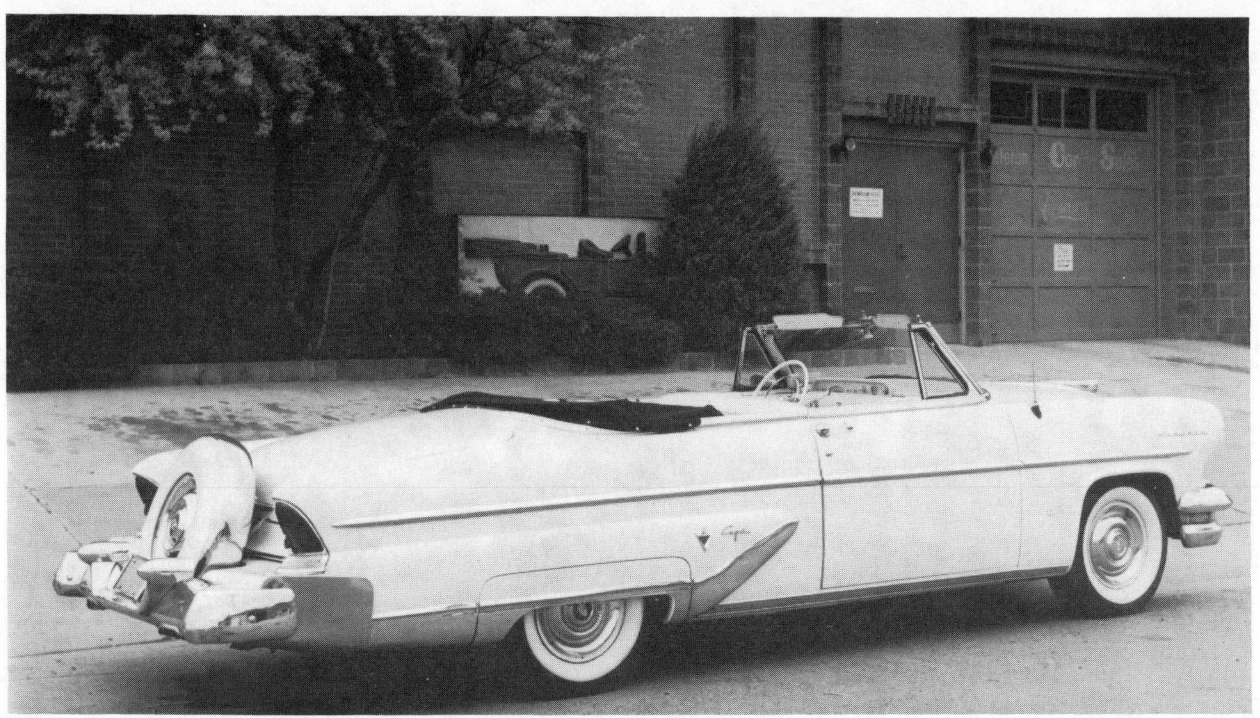

Fig. 2-10. A 1955 Lincoln Capri all decked out in chrome and options.

cubes/225 horsepower. Tires are tubeless. Air conditioning is an optional add-on.

The 1956-57 Continental Mark II's were the last of the Continentals as a separate marque. In the years that followed, Continental went on to become top-of-the-line Lincolns. As I said before, though, it is acceptable to consider the Mark II's along with Lincolns of the Fifties.

Possibly the best place to begin with the '56-'57 Mark II is to say that it is beautiful. Not just nice, not just pretty . . . beautiful! It is a classic. I know my use of that word will bring the snobs screaming out of the woodwork, but the Mark II Continental can stand its own against more than a few of the cars listed by the Classic Car Club of America. In fact, since 1965, the CCCA has included the Mark II as one of the chosen (Fig. 2-11).

The Continental Mark II came about as Ford Motor Company's answer to GM's Cadillac. Ford spent, and lost, a lot of

Fig. 2-11. The elegant 1956 Continental Mark II. A beautiful car, but it just couldn't sell in a market where the equally good-looking Thunderbird already existed for a lot lower price.

Fig. 2-12. 1957 Continental, a contemporary classic.

money finding out that the finned wonder couldn't be toppled no matter how good an automobile they built to compete with it.

The Marks are powered by specially tuned 368 CID Lincoln V-8's attached to three-speed Multi-Drive automatic transmissions and 3.07:1 rear ends. Horsepower is in the 300 range.

These cars were the heaviest, at 4,800 pounds, and most expensive in the industry during their two year run. Wheelbase is 126 inches. Overall length is 218 inches.

Continental Mark II failed to do what Ford had hoped: in spite of all the wonder and respect the Mark II's commanded, they could not replace the Cadillac with American buyers. What the reasons are, I can't say, but certainly the fact that few buyers were willing to spend $10,000 on an automobile in 1956-57, no matter how good it was, has a great deal to do with it (Fig. 2-12). The car that replaced it in 1958 isn't even worth talking about.

MERCURY

Mercury in the Fifties hit two high points in design and managed to be selected as the Indy Pace Car twice. My own first memory of a Fifties Merc goes back to the first time I saw James Dean in "Rebel Without a Cause." His wheels were supplied by Mercury. Like everybody else, I was impressed by the cat in the red nylon jacket and the big, bulbous Merc with the custom look.

The 1950-51 Mercury is similar in style to its well-heeled brother, the Lincoln, but somehow, the Mercury comes off as

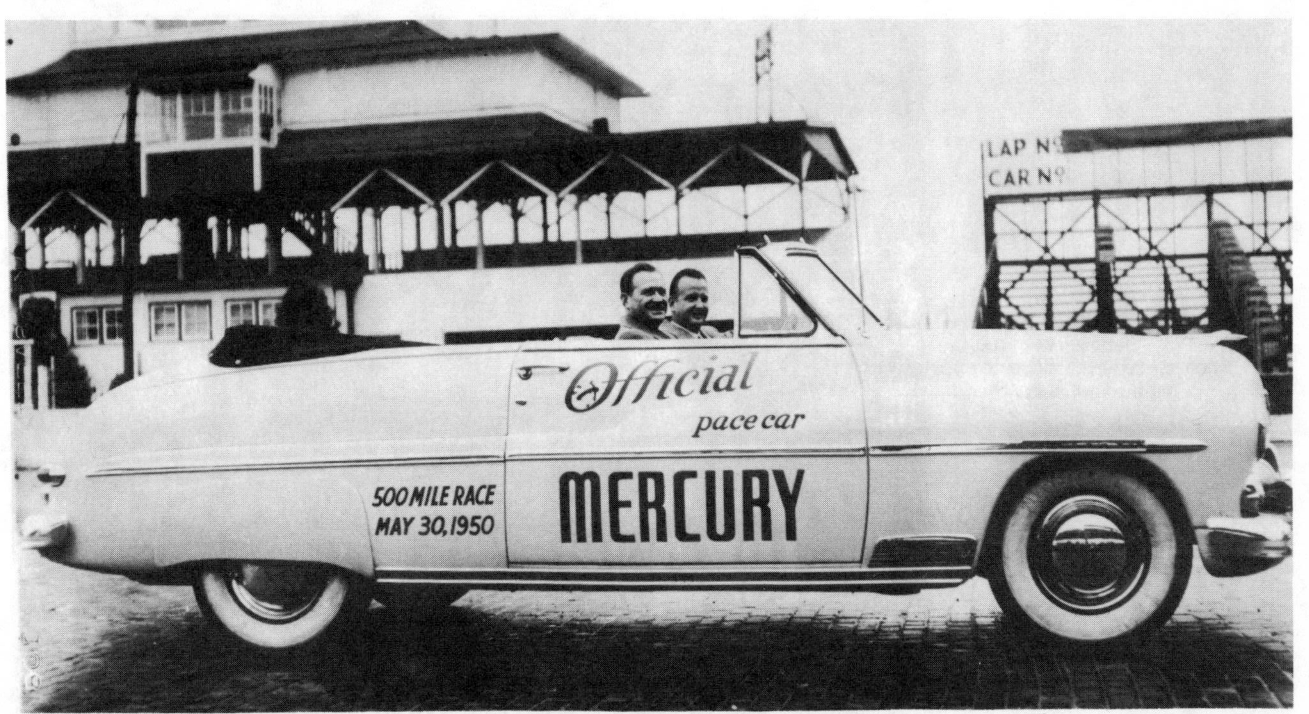

Fig. 2-13. The 1950 Indianapolis 500 Pace Car, a Mercury. The passenger is three time Indy winner Wilbur Shaw. (Wilbur won in 1937, '39 and '40.)

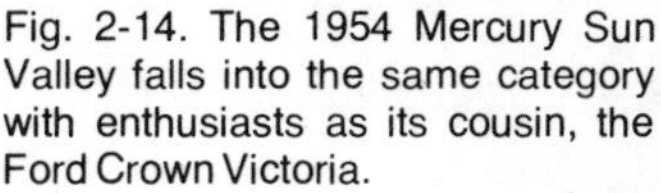

Fig. 2-14. The 1954 Mercury Sun Valley falls into the same category with enthusiasts as its cousin, the Ford Crown Victoria.

better looking. So what if it cost less—the convertible and limited production Monterey coupe with either canvas or leather padded roof are the most popular models today. Major recognition was given to Mercury in 1950 when the convertible was picked to pace at Indy (Fig. 2-13).

The 1950 Merc sits on a 118-inch wheelbase. Power is delivered via a 255 cube, 110 horsepower flat-head V-8.

The 1951 Merc is almost the same car. Grille and bumper arrangement changed slightly. Rear fenders are elongated. Cubic inches for the engine are the same. There are two more available horses. The biggest difference is that you could have your 1951 Merc delivered with two-speed Merc-O-Matic automatic transmission.

If you pick up a stock 1950-51 Mercury, don't expect too much in the way of performance. Do know however, that by hopping up the engine just like they did it back then and tuning your suspension up just a bit, you can have a real goer. Do a little Fifties style custom work and you've got yourself one authentic, true-to-life dreamboat. A lot of purists in the car hobby will say that doing anything non-stock to a car will decrease its value. Bull! If you take care to stick with the period in your modifications, the opposite can easily be true. In maintaining, or even increasing, the value of a car from this decade, period mood is just as important as original equipment. The truth of these statements can best be seen in some of the current examples of the 1950-51 Mercury.

The next generations of Mercuries, beginning in 1952, are bargain dollar Lincolns. Styling and progress in general are virtually the same. The main difference is that the big, expensive Lincolns far outshadow their less distinctive cousins.

Fig. 2-15. A 1957 two-door hardtop Mercury Turnpike Cruiser.

Fig. 2-16. The 1957 Mercury pace car transports that year's queen around the brick yard at Indy.

All that changed in 1954. Mercuries still look like Lincolns of a different color, but they begin to take on an interesting personality of their own. Most notable of the '54 Mercuries is the Sun Valley (Fig. 2-14).

Sun Valley is actually little more than a Monterey option. It consists mainly of the same see-through plastic panel that adorns Ford Skyliners of the same vintage. The intention was to give a somewhat convertible feel to the hardtop car. As with the Skyliner, a shade was included to keep out the rays when the sun got too hot. (The problem with this supposedly better idea is that the see-through roof acts like a greenhouse. In a convertible you have the air flow to keep you comfortable, under glass, you just cook.) Sun Valley roof panels were available in a choice of two different greens or a yellow. Only a few buyers put themselves in a position to make the choice.

The Sun Valley was offered again, in 1955, this time in the Montclair series which replaced Monterey at the top of the line. Again, sales were low. The Sun Valley was out of the line-up for 1956.

A good piece of information to arm yourself with is that the plastic roof inserts didn't wear very well, so even if you find a Sun Valley, the top may be shot. Fortunately, these units are still available here and there NOS (new old stock) or reproduction.

Mercury got its own bodywork for the first time in 1957. The new bodywork is not pretty. Somehow, in spite of the new, unattractive shell, these cars have come to be considered dreamboats by modern enthusiasts (Fig. 2-15).

Perhaps what makes them desirable is that a convertible was chosen to pace at Indy in '57; a big plus ever since the Indy 500 first started (Fig. 2-16).

Or maybe contemporary popularity rests with the 1955 Mercury Turnpike Cruiser. Certainly the name is right; one of the best car names ever. Turnpike Cruisers entered the Mercury line at the top. They were offered new in two and four-door hardtop form and as a convertible. What makes these radical creations special is a bunch of Fifties nonsense. There are twin air intakes and a radio-antenna above the windshield. Seat O Matic automatically adjusted the pilot's seat to your choice of 49 programmed positions. Headlights come in groups of four. The convertibles are Indy pace car replicas. Engines are 290 hp V-8s. The transmission is push button Merc-O-Matic. Enough said.

Chapter 3 Corvette And Thunderbird

Two cars of the Fifties combine to create a phenomenon apart from everything else that went on during that fabulous decade. Those cars are the Chevrolet Corvette and the Ford Thunderbird.

The Corvette was conceived more or less as a sports car and has gone on to become a popular personal car. The Thunderbird was conceived as a popular personal car and has gone on to become one of the great "so-whats" of this century's final years.

Both cars, at some point in their history, enjoyed true sports car handling and power. The day they went into production they were recognized as something quite out of the ordinary. During their golden years, Corvette (1956-57) and Thunderbird (1955-57) enjoyed what can only be considered classic styling. Today enthusiasts and collectors appreciate them for all of those qualities that put them in the class of great cars and grande marques.

The value of these machines continues to escalate rapidly, putting them always near the top of the price scale. Buying one is still a good investment because, like premium stocks, you may have to pay through the nose to get one, but it is one of the surest investments you are likely to make. They are perhaps the only two cars of the Fifties of which every single one made prior to 1960 has considerable collector value. In the case of the Thunderbird collectibility continues on into the Sixties, and as far as Corvette is concerned, many enthusiasts consider even the last models hot properties.

When new, the Corvette and Thunderbird were direct competitors. They share many obvious similarities, and many unique differences.

Chevy and sports car lovers will pick the Vette every time; Ford and luxury car afficianados will go for the 'Bird. I've been fortunate enough to spend several hours behind the wheel of either car under an extreme variety of circumstances and, given the choice between two perfect examples, I probably wouldn't be able to make up my mind.

It isn't difficult to understand what collectors and enthusiasts see in them. They are fine cars; during their golden years, they were probably the best mass production cars in the United States. So let's take a look at them; where they came from, what makes them tick, what's different about them and what they have in common.

CORVETTE

If you take a look at 10 different books, you are likely to find 10 variations on why and how the Corvette came to be. Whether it was developed because some spoiled Detroit brat wanted a sports car to take to college, or whether it was part of Harley Earl's continuing efforts to streamline the automobile, doesn't really matter. The important part of the story begins with a young GM designer named Bob McClean. He was given the assignment of develping a sports-type car. McClean went one better and came up with a true sports car.

He started by placing the car's compact seating area as close as possible to the special rear axle, wheel and tire group. A standard six cylinder Chevy engine was drawn in and just in front of that went the front axle.

This was not a new way of designing a car; it was the way European sports cars had been designed for some time. It was just new to Detroit. Once Harley Earl understood the concept, he decided that this was the correct way to design the car that would become the Corvette. Because of Earl's decision, the first Corvettes were sports cars rather than a chopped and channelled Chevrolet like the Corvair. (It is interesting to note that one of the first names suggested for the car was Corvair.)

Once the rough design was accepted, work began on developing the final working drawings for the body, frame and interior, following British and European styling designs.

A lot of work had to be done in a small amount of time if Corvette was to be ready for its 1953 introduction. When you have the people to get a job done, though, you can do just about anything: the Corvette debuted at the 1953 GM Motorama (Fig. 3-1).

The first Corvette was, and still is, a sight to behold. Born as an entirely new kind of American car, when it's placed next to the Buick Skylark, Cadillac Eldorado and Oldsmobile Fiesta of the same year, it fit right in.

The distinct sports car look starts up front with a full, rounded line and fender mounted headlights covered by wide mesh screens. The line continues to flow to the back of the door, then rises and begins a new curve down and around. At the top of the rear fender, a unique fin of sorts shoots straight back to end in a taillight. A strip of chrome, broken at the wheel wells, travels along the entire side of the car to create an overall pleasing look. Only the chrome strip and the full wheel covers seem out of place for a true sports car—but—the chrome is modest and the wheel covers do sport fake spinners. And those white wall tires . . . oh well. The 102-inch wheelbase is just right.

Powerplant in the '53 'Vette is the worked-over 235 cube Blue Flame six, dishing out 150 horsepower at 4,200 revs (Fig. 3-2). There are aluminum pistons, 8:1 compression ratio, a new camshaft and dual spring valves. If that isn't enough, there are three side-draft Carter single barrel carbs mounted on an aluminum manifold.

In the choice of transmissions, the sports car crowd gets a slap in the face. There is the expected floor mounted shifter, but it

Fig. 3-1. In 1953 Chevrolet began building the Corvette. While the little two-seater shown here faintly resembles the machines of the same name built today, the tradition has been kept up for the most part.

Fig. 3-2. Here's a peek at what the Corvette's first powerplant looked like. These Blue Flame Specials mounted with triple carbs are super rare today and will bring a mint in the hobby marketplace.

controls Chevrolet's two-speed Powerglide transmission instead of what would seem a much more practical three or four-speed manual. That fact is that the Powerglide was the practical choice for Corvette in 1953. GM engineers defended their decision to use the automatic by saying that this kind of application was the coming wave.

One of the things that makes Corvette the special car it is, even in its very latest incarnation, is the glass-reinforced plastic (GRP) body shell. Yes, of course, it breaks upon heavy impact. On the other hand, it doesn't rust and the savings in weight help to make each and every Corvette a muscle car. GRP is liable to show stress cracks after a period of a few years, but the caring enthusiast usually takes care of the problem before it becomes extreme. If you are out looking for a Fifties 'Vette, you aren't likely to find one that doesn't show some stress cracking. As long as it isn't too extreme, don't worry about it, just get it taken care of when the 'Vette finally belongs to you.

An interesting side note to the production of the Corvette is the original marketing strategy. From the beginning, until mid-1954, GM promoted the Corvette as a "VIP-only" car. The Corvette, GM execs thought, would receive the best attention if it sold only to prestige owners. That meant if you were a movie star, a retired general, a millionaire or some sort of royalty, you could plunk down $3,513 and have the white (they were all white—and the customers probably were too for that matter) Corvette of your choice. If you were Milt the Mechanic down at Tony's Texaco, no price could get you a 'Vette.

It didn't take long for this act of incredible stupidity to prove a failure. In 1953, 300 Corvettes were built. Some 180 of them were sold. After all, what member of the above-mentioned groups wanted an American roadster that wasn't as pretty, powerful or prestigious as its European counterparts? Not to mention the leaky side curtains.

The 1954 Corvette is virtually the same car as the '53 except for a few changes that helped make 1954 a considerably better sales year. First, Chevrolet decided to dump its prestige buyer plan. Second, Corvettes were offered in a small variety of colors in addition to good old Polo White. You could get your '54 Vette in Pennant Blue, Sportsman Red and Jet Black; all better looking on the car than white, even though white is about the only color of 1953-55 Vette you usually see (Fig. 3-3).

Also for 1954, exhaust pipes exit from below rather than out of the lower rear body. Some later '54 engines got a hot cam that boosted horsepower to 155. On some '54 engines you will find some chrome, most notably, the rocker covers. Just under 3,000 units were sold.

As with the rest of the Chevrolet line, things got hopping for the Corvette in 1955. If you look at the body of the car, you won't see much difference between it and its predecessors. Nevertheless, some mid-Fifties magic was performed on the '55 Vette in the form of Chevy's new V-8 and in the person of one Zora Arkus Duntov (Fig. 3-4).

Duntov brought to the Corvette his European sense of just what a sports car should be. It was this European attitude that made the 1955-57 Vettes true sports cars. The first change Duntov made was to tune up what could only be called the sloppy handling of the Corvette. A few minor suspension changes brought the Vette up to European sports car handling standards and also took care of a good share of the Corvette's overall performance problems.

Just one thing was missing, an engine that would change Corvette's getaway performance from pussycat to Puma. Tabby's a fine little cat, but it takes muscle to become the king of the jungle. That muscle came to Corvette via Chevy's new 265 CID V-8 of 195 horsepower. Performance of the '55 Vette is exciting: 0-60 in eight to nine seconds. If you're lucky enough to find one of the handful of

Fig. 3-3. The 1954 Corvette. To many enthusiasts, this is the Vette's truest sports car form.

'55 Vettes that were built with the manual, three-speed transmission, it'll move out even quicker than that.

Now the bad news. Thanks to a reputation for so-so performance that wouldn't die and competition from Ford's beautiful Thunderbird, Corvette sales continued their downhill run. At a base price of $2,800-$2,950, only 700 1955 Corvettes were sold.

The Corvette was born in 1953. In 1954, it was an awkward child. By 1955, it had reached puberty. And in 1956, the Corvette came of age. In the face of an impending corporate execution, big daddy Ed Cole kept the Corvette alive and pushed it through sales of more than 3,000 copies. With Thunderbird out there cruising as undisputed king of the boulevard, Cole made the decision to carry the Corvette forward yet another step as a sports car of the first magnitude.

The body of the 1956 Corvette shows direct descendence from the first generation although completely restyled. One immediately notices the similarity between the '56 Vette and European sports of the day.

Where the front fender line of the earlier Vettes flows around and back, the line of the '56 shoots forward, accentuated by headlights that are mounted out rather than inset. A bullet-shaped, concave side panel from the back of the front wheel wells to just behind mid-door give the '56 Vette an even more streamlined look. The rear fender line wraps around as it had previously, but the

Fig. 3-4. In 1955, form and function began to catch up with each other as the V-8 engine became an option and the suspension got seriously reconsidered.

Fig. 3-5. Here are front (A) and rear (B) views of what, in my opinion, is the finest Corvette ever produced. As you can see from the license plate, it's a '57. The machine that Chevrolet produced in 1957 is so good that the company could still be building them without change and have an excellent automobile.

taillight appendages are gone. Taillights are now nicely inset. Every line, every curve of the '56 Vette looks right. The result is the most attractive (with its twin of '57) Corvette ever built.

An optional hardtop for inclement weather driving, roll up windows (now it's a convertible, not a roadster) and a power operated convertible top were all added in '56.

If that ain't enough to suit ya', as the saying goes, then some Duntov touches should do the trick. First, he put in a new high lift cam and brought the 265 cube power plant up to 225 horses at 5,200 rpm. Then, he threw in a manual transmission. At full tilt, the 1956 Vette will do something like 115-125 mph and 0-60 in under eight seconds. Carburetion on the '56 could be had in the form of either one or two four-barrels.

Outside of the engine and body, Corvette was made a better car in 1956 by Duntov's beefing up of the frame and suspension. With the changes that had already been made in 1955, it didn't take a whole hell of a lot to make the '56 even better.

With all the revising and restyling that took place prior to the introduction of the new Corvette in 1956, Chevy's glass bomb had become a great car. Today, postwar car enthusiasts consider the 1956 (and 1957) Vette a period classic. That, plus its milestone status, puts a premium on the car's current value, but it's worth it. The price of these cars isn't likely to ever go down.

Visually, the 1957 Corvette looks like the '56. Indeed, it is much the same car. Except, that is, for three little things; engine, transmission and rear end (Fig. 3-5).

Beginning with the rear, you have a choice of rear axles, including one with a 4.11:1 ratio. In the middle of the car, the folks at Chevrolet finally planted a real live (optional) four-speed with ratios of 2.20:1, 1.66:1, 1.31:1 and 1:1.

That's all neat, but the biggest and best improvement of all came in the form of a brand spanking new 283 CID, small block V-8 engine, every bit the performer its daddy was. The new, bigger engine came out of the factory capable of anywhere from 220 to 283 horsepower, depending on what method you chose to get fuel into the engine. Start with one four-barrel carburetor. If that isn't sufficient go for two fours. And for those who would rule the world, Chevrolet offered fuel injection as an option. Using the most powerful choice available, Chevy came up with its famous one cubic inch equals one horsepower slogan. (There is a good deal of evidence to suggest that the 283 Chevy mill equipped with fuel injection is capable of closer to 300 horsepower, but 283 = 283 sounds better in the advertising.)

There were also some Corvette suspension improvements that make the '57 unique. An excellent handling package included heavier springs, heavy-duty shocks, front anti-roll bar, metallic brake linings, finned drum brakes, quicker steering and positraction.

Naturally, 1957 sales reflected the improvement of the breed. At a base price of $3,465, some 6,339 units were built. The Vette was catching on.

Unfortunately though, the Vette wasn't catching on quite fast enough to suit GM brass. So, in 1958, the Corvette went the way of so many other Fifties cars. In that year, the ultra clean American sports car became an overdecorated, boulevard cruising dream-boat. Don't laugh, sports car lovers; this model sold almost 3,000 more copies than the '57.

First the headlights multiplied and took on the gimmicky 2×2 look. Instead of just blending into the fender, they are surrounded by a chrome strip. A narrow strip of chrome tops the fender directly behind the chrome headlight bezels. A new smaller opening was placed on either side of the grille, all, surrounded by chrome. Fake reverse air scoops are mounted behind the front wheel wells. Three narrow chrome strips exit from each of them. A row of 18 fake louvers covers the hood. The Corvette's 1958 body is about 10 unnecessary inches longer that the '57, and is finished off with more chrome at the back of the car.

Other changes for 1958 were more in line with years previous. Fuel injection got even better, developing an advertised 290 horses, and became more dependable. The double four-barrel version kicked out a not-too-shabby 270 horsepower.

The 1958 Vette's interior is where the biggest improvement shows up. A console was placed between two narrower, but perfectly acceptable seats. The dashboard is a huge improvement. For the first time in a Corvette, all gauges are mounted in the traditional, more practical position directly in front of the driver.

Little difference is found between the '58 Vette and the '59. Thankfully, hood and rear deck are stripped of 1958 affectations. 1959 is considered the year the Corvette began to shift over to what it became in the final third of the century: a sporty, luxury, personal car (Fig. 3-6). If you wanted a sports car, Duntov made the proper goodies available. But a trend was starting, and most people who bought Corvettes since then have done it because they want to feel like they're driving a luxury touring car and look like they're driving a sports car.

To this day, the Corvette survives, not too awfully far removed from its original intention. Afterall, it's still sporty, still a two-seater and, by modern standards, still fairly powerful. That's a lot more than can be said for the Thunderbird nameplate that began

Fig. 3-6. By 1959, Chevrolet was trying to fit Corvette into the automobile mainstream, slowly moving away from the true sports car theme of '53-57.

A fabric top whisks into place in seconds—
to protect you from sudden rainstorms. It's
completely out of sight when not in use.
Thunderbird

Fig. 3-7. This ad is one of the rare reminders of what the first Thunderbird was intended to look like. Last minute changes included the removal of the chrome side trim. Some enthusiasts believe a few cars were actually built with the side trim, but I doubt it. If I'm wrong, and one or two of these exist, they will be worth considerably more than regular 55's.

life so gallantly and has, in its most recent form, become a rolling joke.

THUNDERBIRD

In 1951 (yes, 1951) Ford brass started thinking about a two-seater all their own. In 1952, designers and engineers were told to have one ready for 1955 model introduction. Shortly after that, the Ford brass, along with everybody else, got to see the new GM two seater at the 1953 Motorama. It was suddenly obvious that the competition had a headstart and there was nothing to do but go ahead with building their very own little car. In early 1953, Ford brass passed down the word to proceed at speed with the two-seater project.

From the very beginning, Ford was talking about a different kind of car than the Corvette. Rule number one: The Ford two-seater must have the same straight line as other contemporary Fords. This was akin to saying, "Whatever you do, don't design a Ford sports car!" GM was trying to build a sports car; it would be up to Ford to build something so entirely different that the two wouldn't possibly be considered alike. A personal car! That's what the two-seat Ford would be. And so it was. The personal car, the boulevard cruiser, was born. Design was intended to provide both comfort and performance.

As the project neared completion, it was time to give the two-seater a name. Sportsman, El Tigre, Sport Liner, Arcturus and Coronado all were suggested. Firebird was not only suggested, but only missed being chosen by a hair. Thunderbird, however, had just the right ring to it. Thunderbird it was (Fig. 3-7).

The first Thunderbird made its premiere at the Detroit Auto Show in February, 1954. With a few minor design changes, this is the same car that began rolling off the assembly line on September 9, 1954. At first glance, the Thunderbird looked entirely unique. A second look revealed that necessary straight line. A closer look yet revealed to the astute contemporary viewer a two-seat car that looked like a miniature Fairlane. The Thunderbird was lower, shorter, sportier, but the family resemblance was clear emphasized by the stip of chrome body trim that ran along the side of the first Thunderbird. It was identical to that on the '55 Fairlane. (That chrome strip was removed before the Thunderbird entered production).

There are enthusiasts and collectors who claim that several production Thunderbirds came off the line with the Fairlane trim.

Fig. 3-8. 1955: The first Thunderbird. Boulevardeer, not sports car. Slim, sleek, beautiful, it was an immediate success.

This is a rather exciting rumor that has never been verified, but the earliest Thunderbird ads did show the car with the Fairlane trim. I won't venture an opinion. If such a car exists, it would probably bring a premium of $5,000 or more over the current value of standard Thunderbirds.

As the Corvette edged ever closer to becoming a true sports car, the first Thunderbirds were introduced as much more civilized machines. Not only did the Thunderbird not look like other Fifties sports cars, it came with a list of options that would make the rough-and-ready sports car purists shudder. There was power steering, power brakes, power seat, an opera type hardtop and roll up windows. A Fordomatic three-speed automatic was intended as standard equipment, but if you were among the more rugged Thunderbird buyers, you could get a tree-speed manual with overdrive.

Getting back to the look of the first Thunderbirds, even on a car that was intended to use mostly standard Ford components, a few things had to be unique. Most noticeably, there is the super attractive eggcrate grille. Below that is a small, attractive bumper with large twin ornaments looking like nothing in particular, but stylish. To the rear, large round taillights are topped by small chrome triangles. While the straight Ford line is preserved, these taillights and triangles give the Thunderbird a finned look (Fig. 3-8).

The 1955 Thunderbirds carry 3,200 pounds on their short 102-inch wheelbase. This weight could be shaved down considerably if a few of the luxury appointments were left off.

A 292 CID V-8 develops 198 horsepower at 4400 rpm with an 8.5:1 compression ratio. A single four-barrel carburetor is mounted. For looks, the engine carries special Thunderbird valve covers and air cleaner. The '55 Thunderbird suspension is the victim of the edict that stated that as many parts as possible had to be standard Ford. As you might guess, what works for one car might not for another. If you keep your Bird at 55 mph or less and mind all the signs, you'll probably do just fine. Any attempts at creative driving will put you in trouble (Fig. 3-9).

For 1956, Thunderbird received a few minor styling changes. On the front fender, just ahead of the door, a small air vent is added. Those small triangles above the taillights became back up lights in '56. The spare tire for Thunderbird's second year has been moved to the outside, enclosed in a continental kit. This not only gives the Bird a very nifty look, it also makes a bunch of extra room

Fig. 3-9. The dash for '55—and following years—was luxury car, rather than sports car stark. Very few Birds of '55 were produced with the floor shift you see here.

in the trunk (Fig. 3-10). The final outward change to the '56 Bird is in the hardtop. To enhance visibility and add a touch of class, the '56 got a round opera window (Fig. 3-11).

Under the hood, the '56 Bird was updated from the '55, too. The 292 cuber with its 202 horses came only with the three-speed stick. Fordomatic and overdrive equipped cars came with a couple of options: first, there is the 312 cube, 215/225 (overdrive/automatic) horsepower V-8, then there's the Thunderbird power pack. This is the hot item to look for if you're in the market for a '56 Bird. It consists of a hotter cam and a pair of four-barrel carburetors and 245 fire-breathing horses. Handling improved, but not greatly.

Like the rest of the Ford line, the Thunderbird was completely restyled for 1957 (Fig. 3-12). Up front the biggest change came in the bumper/grille area. On the '55 and '56 Birds, bumper and grille are distinctly separate pieces. On the 1957 Bird, both are combined into one big, heavy assembly. To the rear (actually beginning on the door), Thunderbirds of '57 vintage carry fins (Fig. 3-13). Big round taillights continue the tradition, but those little triangles are replaced by the fins. Parking lights are now integral in

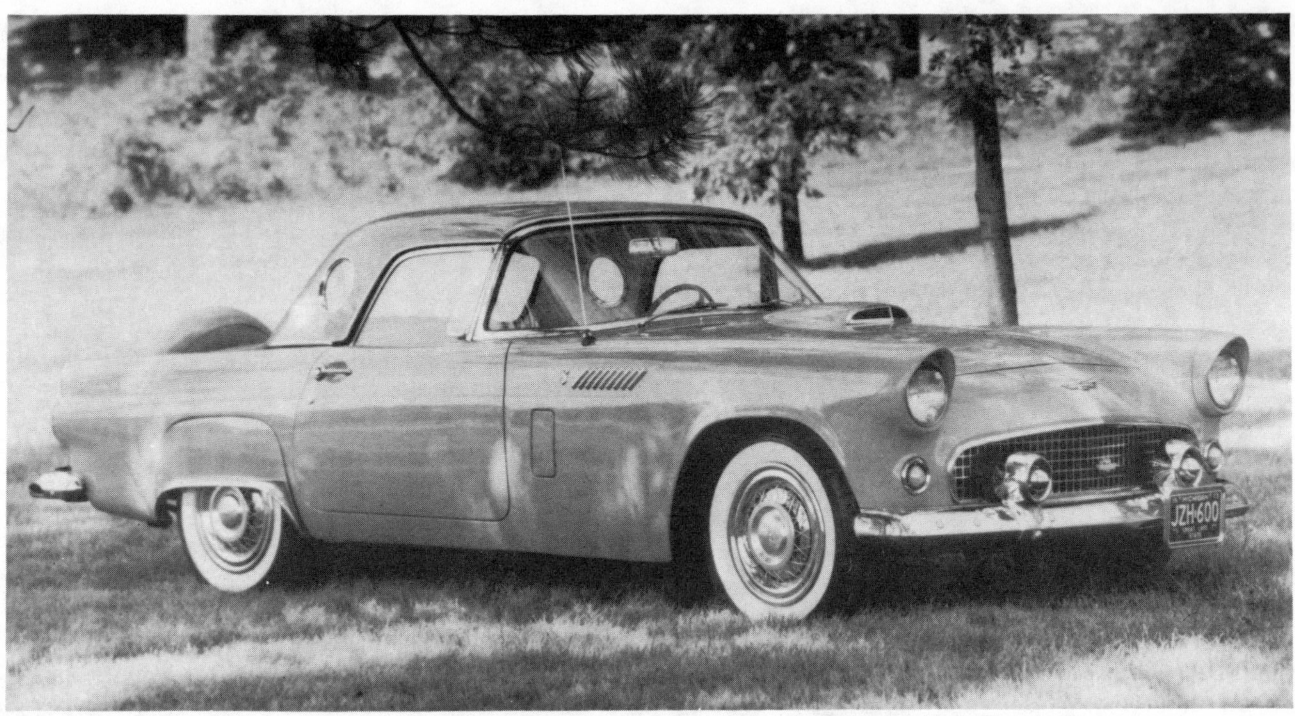

Fig. 3-10. The big Bird changes for 1956 were a vent door, a porthole and an exterior mounted spare tire.

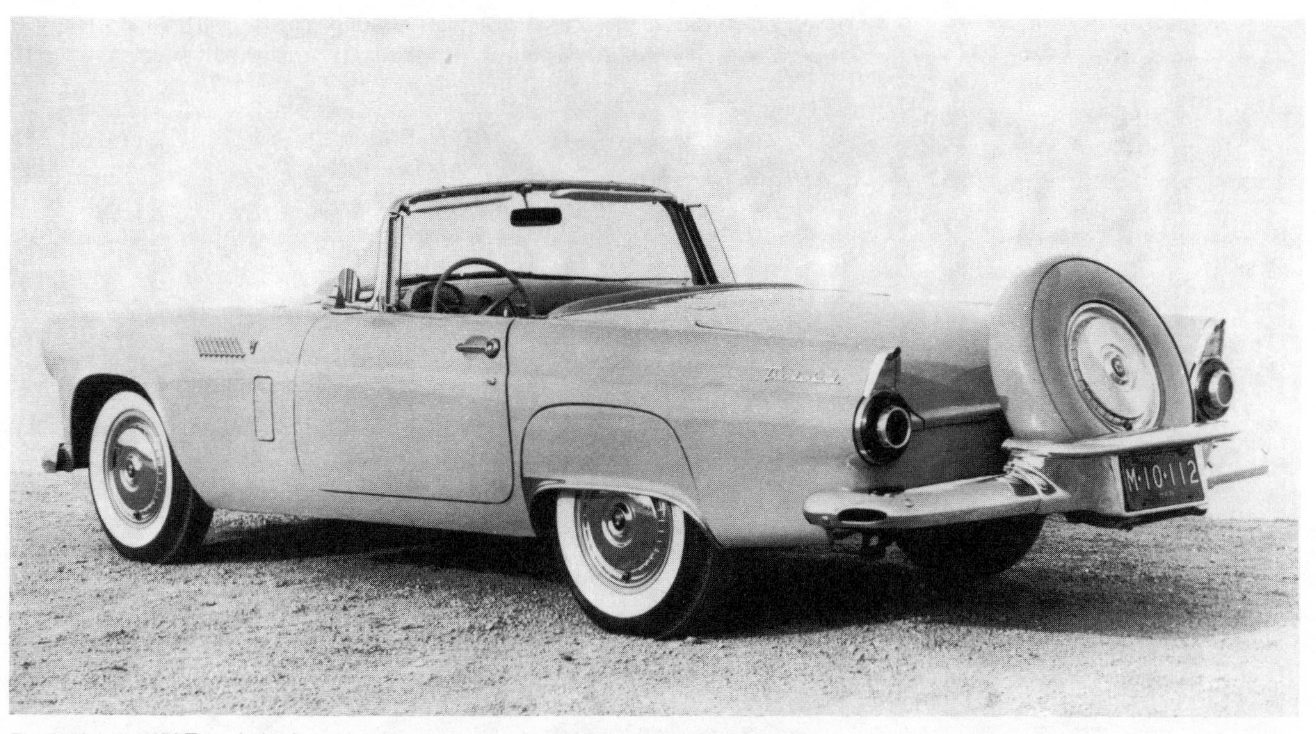

Fig. 3-11. In this '56 Thunderbird photo, notice the exhausts exiting through the rear bumper.

Fig. 3-12. For 1957, the Thunderbird grew fins, but there was nothing unattractive about them.

Fig. 3-13A & B. The '57 Bird is elegant from bumper-to-bumper and road-to-roof.

the taillights. The rear bumper is free of the conny kit from '56 and dual exhaust exit through it.

In the same year that Corvettes got fuel injection, Thunderbirds got something special of their own for blowing the slow pokes off the street: a supercharger that came along and put 300 horsepower hairs on the chest of the 312 CID V-8. If you find a Bird with one of these babies in it, you've found gold. If supercharging didn't suit the buyer circa 1957, you could also get dual fours or even one four-throat pots.

The slowest 1957 Thunderbird will do at least 100 mph. The fastest is capable of almost 130. The suspension was once again improved, but not near enough to make the Bird an honest to goodness road car (Fig. 3-14).

For my money, the poor handling characteristics of the 1955-57 Thunderbird have been overstressed by too many automotive writers. Virtually all of them are comparing it to Corvettes and European sports cars of the same period. In those circles it can't compete. Like I said, it just isn't a real sports car. It wasn't

Fig. 3-14. The 1957 Thunderbird was a peak in good looks. It remains a symbol of the good life today.

Fig. 3-15. When 1958 rolled around, a new Thunderbird made the scene. Purists are still cussing, but today the squareBird has a large following all its own.

intended to be. The Thunderbird was planned as a kind of two-seat luxury car, designed to look sharp and provide a ride that felt good. Considering the classic Birds in these terms, it's one damn good car.

In 1958, Ford created the square Bird (Fig. 3-15). Aficionados of sports and personal cars cringed as the boys from Detroit created blasphemy by turning the beautiful little two-seater into a big car. Why, the bloody thing'll seat four people! How personal, how sporty, can that be? The purists hated the car when it was new and they hate it today.

To another, larger group the 1958 Thunderbird went from neat little car that they could never own, to a car with a sporty name and history and big enough to carry the wife and kids. The car made its appearance as an authentic nifty Fifties dreamboat. People loved it. Judging from the way the '58 (and '59) Thunderbird has attracted modern day enthusiasts and collectors, I'd say they still love it.

All that remained from the classic Birds were the fins (same), hood scoop (wider) and the taillights (four of them). The '58 is longer, wider, full of chrome and options. The grille is similar, but heavier. Headlights are doubled. Every clean sweeping line has been junked. The wide, flat deck is broken by a stylized sunken area at its center.

The Thunderbird was always considered a luxury car. With the introduction of the '58 model, it became a big luxury car. And it sold! It sold almost 38,000 copies in a combination of convertible and hardtop forms. There were more options made available in 1958-59 than any sane person could want or afford. The standard engine went up to 352 cubes in 1958. In '59, the car came with a big 430 CID boat anchor as standard equipment.

The square Birds are two feet longer and 1,000 pounds heavier than '57. Wheelbase is almost a foot longer. Why, when they already had a popular car, did the Ford brass decide to change it? Apparently, the reasoning was that more room was needed for family oriented car buyers. In that sense the addition of a rear seat greatly expanded the car's sales potential. Clearly, Ford management figured the newer models appealed to a broader segment of the public.

As usual, "more is better" became the operative phrase. The little car with character and soul had, by the end of the decade, become a glittering, chromed and finned dreamboat.

So, whoever said Detroit had a heart?

The 1950 Oldsmobile 88.

1953 Nash-Healey.

A 1954 Kaiser . . .

And the 1954 Lincoln Capri.

The 1955 Ford Crown Victoria.

The 1955 Chrysler Windsor.

The ever-popular 1956 Chevrolet.

Top rivals of the '50's: the 1957 Thunderbird . . .

And the 1957 Corvette.

A 1957 Pontiac Bonneville.

Pure luxury: the 1958 Cadillac Eldorado Brougham.

The 1959 DeSoto Adventurer.

959's Chrysler 300E.

The Arnolt-Bristol.

Chapter 4 Chrysler Corporation

During the Fifties, the several divisions of Chrysler Corporation built cars that covered the whole spectrum of buyers. You could get them with all the power, chrome and fins you could possibly want. They came top down, top up, sleek or stocky. Or, you could pick up the biggest, most boring family sedan built in the United States of America.

When today's enthusiasts think of Chrysler cars from the Fifties, they don't think of boring. They think about the fastest cars of the decade. They talk about the most heavily chromed and finned cars of the decade. The most knowledgeable enthusiasts talk about the three Indy pace cars produced by Chrysler Corporation during the Fifties; 1951 Chrysler New Yorker, 1956 De Soto Fireflite and 1954 Dodge Royal.

Even though many enthusiasts are well aware of Chrysler Corporation's accomplishments during the decade, the cars have generally gotten a bad rap from John Q. Public. The fact is that among this breed, the enthusiast and collector can find some of the most dependable cars of the Fifties and some of today's best hobby car buys.

Beginning with the corporation's namesake, let's take a look at each division independently.

CHRYSLER

Compared to other auto makers, Chrysler entered the Fifties on the wrong foot. Oh, the cars may have been just right for Aunt

Myrtle or Sister Mary Catherine. But the person who wanted a car that went like scat and looked like a dreamboat, they just wouldn't do . . . with two exceptions that is. The first, the 1950 Chrysler Town & Country hardtop the most sought after postwar American automobiles. Only about 700 of these handsome machines were manufactured at a cost of around $4,000. If you're thinking that isn't cheap, you're right. In 1950 dollars, that was a whole lot of money. One in very good condition today will easily bring over $10,000. We have heard of offers being made at amounts double and triple that (Fig. 4-1).

The Town & Country of 1950 is not the same car as the 1949 and earlier models, but it is still an eye pleasing automobile. This flashy Newport hardtop no longer carries mahogany veneer or a completely wood finished panel. Instead, ash trim is bolted onto the unadorned steel body. To the enthusiast (lucky fellow) who already has one of the earlier Town & Countries, the 1950 version may not look like much. To someone with a less biased view, however, the ash-trimmed 1950 Town & Country Newport hardtop stands out as an extremely attractive example of Forties influence on the wildest decade in automobile design (Fig. 4-2).

The '50 Town & Countries are powered by a straight eight of 323 cubic inches and 135 horsepower. The car sits on a 131.5-inch

Fig. 4-1. Artist Bruce Bingham's rendition of perhaps the mot collectible of all Fifties Chryslers, the 1950 T & C.

Fig. 4-2. In 1950, the Town and Country was stripped of some of its wood, but Chrysler still advertised it as a "Thoroughbred."

wheelbase. My only criticism of the visual presentation of the car would be that already in 1950, it showed Chrysler's trend toward excess, by overdoing the chrome. Where the wood trim should be allowed to make its own statement, chrome intrudes. There are chrome strips on front and back fenders that line up (sort of) with the center wood strip. Behind the front wheel well and in front of the rear are splash-guard-like chrome panels. Another panel of chrome curves around from the bumper/grille assembly to the front wheel well. I guess when you consider the fabulous excesses to come, the extra brightwork here isn't all that bad.

The 1950 model is the last of the true Town & Countries. After that the series name continued—on station wagons which carried no wood trim at all—but the spirit was gone.

In 1951, Chrysler introduced its first V-8, a 331 cube, 180 horse powerplant with hemispherical combustion chambers. The mill became known popularly as the Hemi. The name Chrysler gave it was FirePower. Bore and stroke is 3 13/16 x 3⅝. Important to enthusiasts and collectors today is the fact that low octane regular gasoline may be used thanks to the Hemi's lower compression ratio of 7.5:1. As a wheel turner, the Hemi is no slouch. As a quality engine, it ranks with the Ford flathead and Chevy and Ford small blocks as a true milestone.

Unfortunately, the body styles of the first few years of the decade do not match their powerplants in creating excitement among enthusiasts and collectors. They didn't create a lot of enthusiasm when they were new, and they don't do it now either. They are, however, very dependable automobiles that are still very undervalued. For the enthusiast or collector who wants a real nice car and can't afford an out-and-out dreamboat or milestone, these early Fifties Chryslers are one of the best investments going. They ain't pretty, but they ain't ugly either (Fig. 4-3).

The one exception is the Hemi-powered 1951 Chrysler New Yorker convertible. Wheelbase is 131 inches; weight 4,460 pounds. In 1951, you could drive it home for around $4,000; not exactly what would have been considered cheap. Power steering is attached as a first-in-the-industry, hot option.

To be perfectly honest, the only things that make the '51 New Yorker as desirable as it is are its pace car status and the fact that it is a Hemi-powered convertible. So you can bet that an Indy Pace Car replica is the version to look for.

In 1955, Virgil Exner introduced the American car buying public to the "Forward" and "Million Dollar" looks. It was

Fig. 4-3. Chrysler FirePower paced the Indy 500 in 1951.

Fig. 4-4. Every bit as good looking as its brother, the 300, is the 1955 Chrysler Windsor convertible.

Chrysler's ad men who developed the two slogans, but it was chief of design, Exner, who actually created the look.

In addition to the extraordinary Chrysler 300 which I'll get back to, two other outstanding models were produced by Chrysler in 1955. They are, naturally, Windsor and New Yorker. In place of the boxy, boring shapes of previous years, the '55 Chryslers have clean, well-defined lines that create a certain look of power even when the cars are standing still. Exner's space age styling is very much in evidence in the steamlined body and trim (Fig. 4-4).

The look begins with egg crate grilles, divided at center by a V-shaped body panel. A long, unbroken strip of chrome trim runs along the beltline from extreme front to extreme rear where a small chrome fin and tailight housing tops off the slightly sloping rear fender (Fig. 4-5).

For the modern day collector or enthusiast in search of a Windsor or New York, the top choice should be a convertible. Failing that, there are two hardtops for each model to choose from. Both cars sit on a 126-inch wheel-base. The engine provided is a 188 horsepower, 301 CID V-8.

In '56 form, the Windsor and New Yorker look much the same as in '55. Except, that is, for the decided upswing taken by the tail fins and the disappearance of the separation between the grilles, which became, in 1956 one considerably less attractive grille. The 1955 Chryslers in convertible and hardtop form would be considered dreamboats by anyone. But when 1956 came around and those fins shot up, the word dreamboat took on true meaning. With chrome glimmering and engine humming along, here is an automobile to make the car lover's heart go pitter-patter in double time. Again, both Windsor and New Yorker are mounted on a 126-inch wheelbase, but the '56 Windsor carries a 331 cube, 225 horse engine, while the New Yorker boasts the FirePower 354 of 280 horses. Both, you will find, are extremely good highway cruisers (Fig. 4-6).

Now, let's get back to the Chrysler we all really want to talk about, the 300. After all, even in a list of dreamboats and milestones, there are just so many legends.

Visually, the Chrysler 300 looked much like the rest of the Chrysler line from its very beginning in 1955, even though, it kept the divided egg crate grilles one year longer than the other Chryslers.

What really set the 300 apart was its successful competition in a Fifties phenomena called the horsepower race that had been raging since 1949. Then, all of a sudden, in 1955 everybody got dead serious. Chevy introduced a miracle in metal, the 195 horsepower small block. Ford's 272 cube V-8 was developing up to 182 horses. The powerful Cadillac was the most serious contender of all, with a roaring 270 horsepower under the hood. If Chrysler wanted to be a contender in this company, it would have to produce a car capable not only of roaring, but also breathing fire.

Enter the 1955 Chrysler 300. What we have in the first 300 is a 331-cubic-inch Hemi-head V-8 capable of 300 of those fire-breathing horses, thanks to dual four-barrel carbs, a hot cam and solid lifters. The suspension is beefed up to road racing

Fig. 4-5. The all new, all original, 1955 Chrysler 300. A fire breathing horsepower monster.

Fig. 4-6. In 1956, 300 became 300B, adding fins and yet more horsepower.

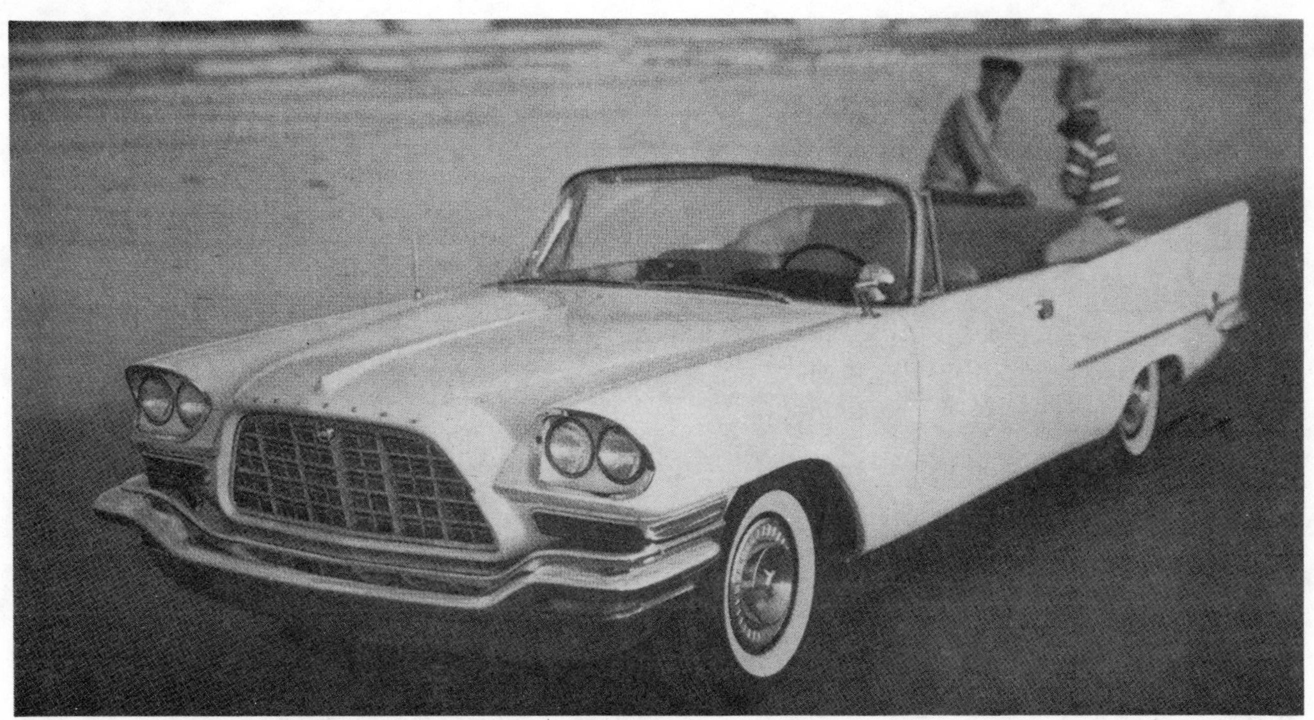

Fig. 4-7. The 1957 Chrysler 300C convertible with 375 horsepower. Watch those fins grow.

capabilities, including heavy duty shocks and stiffer springs. The body is a basic two-door hardtop New Yorker with less ostentatious Windsor trim. The grilles are '55 Imperial. The interior is leather with Imperial touches. When it was new, you could have bought it for a measly $4,055. Try to find one now for that price; don't be surprised if you have to pay better than twice that. With the exception of the very fastest Corvettes, the 300 is the fastest American production automobile made in 1955.

In 1956, 331 cubes grew to 354. Horsepower jumped to 340. As with the rest of the line, styling remained basically the same. Models from '56 are called 300B.

For 1957, things styling became extreme with the 300. The slab sides are among the most decidedly slab-sided of the decade. Fins literally zoom off to the rear (Fig. 4-7). Dual headlights on the '57 300 are among the first in the industry. The one piece grille is large, and despite looking like the open mouth of a large-mouth bass, it is somehow not totally unattractive. In fact, there's a rather large group who call it the most attractive of all Fifties grilles. Going one step further, we have seen several automotive journalists say in print that the car is gracefully finned and modestly grilled; that's a little hard to swallow. On the other hand, I wouldn't disagree for a moment with the enthusiast who calls these cars exciting or even stunning. Breathtaking may be the best way to describe them.

The '57 300C scored big on the sand at Daytona. The standard powerplant delivers 375 horses from its 392 cubes. An optional mill would give you 390 horsepower. It's generally agreed that Exner's design talents reached their highest point in the 1957 Chrysler 300C.

The 300D and 300E of 1958 and '59 are much the same as their immediate predecessor. The '58 came new with either the standard 380 horsepower engine or an optional fuel-injected unit that would put 390 horses at the touch of your foot.

In 1959, the most powerful power source became the 380 horsepower version of Chrysler's new Golden Lion 413, a wedge-head V-8. Compression ratio of the wedge is 10:1. Couple that to a 3.31:1 rear end and TorqueFlite, and you have a version of what has been called the "decline" of the series (Fig. 4-8).

Detractors of the 300E may say what they will. As the decade dimmed, Chrysler 300 was still king of the hill. All 1955-59 300's are certified milestones. Now what was that somebody said about yesterday's heroes and the legends of today?

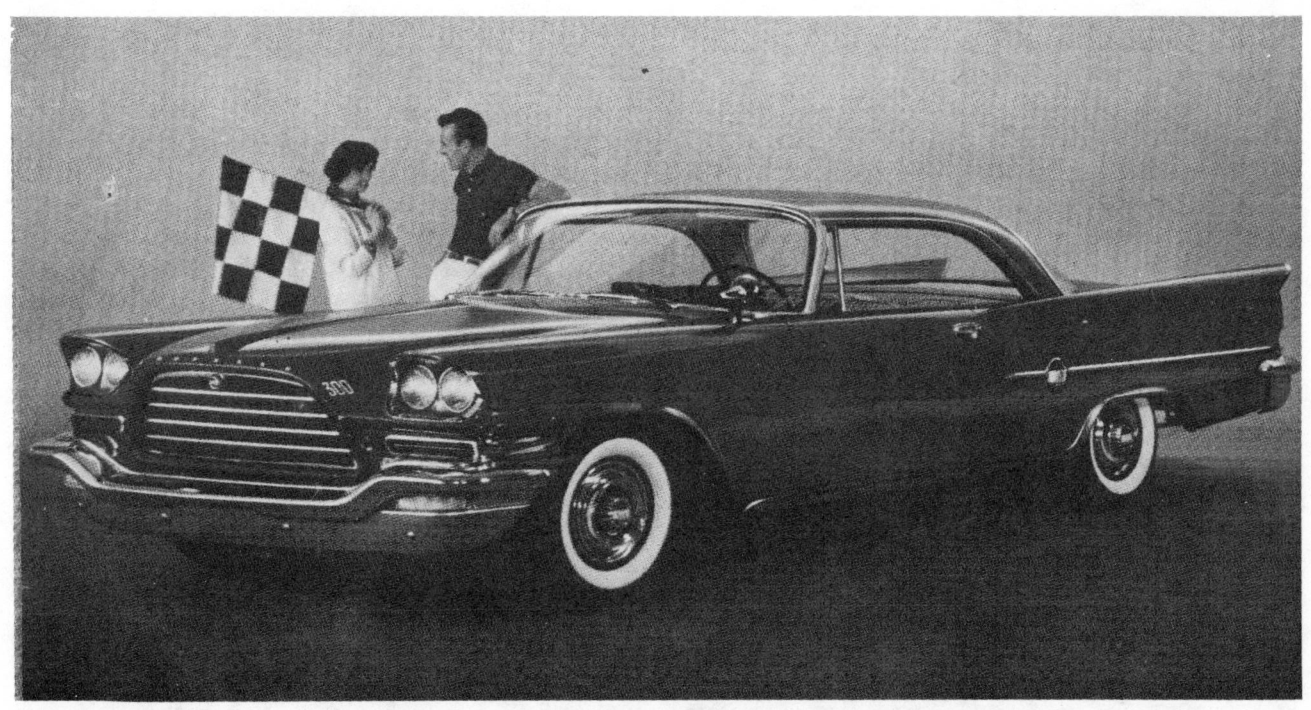

Fig. 4-8. By 1959, the 300, now an E, had lost some of its go-power. Even debeefed though, they are still collected as early muscle cars.

DESOTO

If we're going to talk about DeSoto's under the heading of dreamboats and milestones, we can begin with 1955. Some very good DeSotos were produced prior to that, and they are being collected. But, none of them are certified milestones and to call them dreamboats, you would have to be drunk or drugged.

Current collector interest dictates that the car to start with is the 1955 Fireflite (Fig.4-9). More chrome, more color and no fins immediately distinguish the DeSoto from its Chrysler cousins.

The DeSoto has so much chrome up front that it's almost surprising the things don't tip up on their nose: an all-chrome bumper/grille assembly, above that, DeSoto in good sized chome letters; above that, a weird looking, hood-scoop affair. To the outside edges, headlights and more chrome. Now, just for a touch of class, add brightwork ornamentation to each front fender and one at hood center for balance.

It seems like everything on the Fireflite is outlined in chrome, including the large two-tone color panel and matching roof (on the Sportsman hardtops). With everything else, I suppose, fins might be just a bit too much.

DeSoto shares Chrysler's 126-inch wheelbase. The standard engine in the '55 Fireflite is the 291-cubic-inch, 200 horsepower V-8.

For 1956, DeSoto grew fins. The largest example was found on the Fireflite (and the Adventurer). Wheelbase for the '56 is again, as with Chrysler, 126 inches. Engines could be had in the new DeSotos in a choice of 230 and 255 horsepower versions. Minor facelifting makes the '56 DeSoto a little less attractive than the previous year. The fins are the only difference that really stands out.

A Fireflite paced the Indy 500 in 1956, so if you are looking to make a purchase, the ideal would be a Pace Car replica (Fig. 4-10).

The really hot DeSoto of 1956 vintage is the Adventurer. Introduced that year as DeSoto's answer to the Chrysler 300, the Adventurer was limited in production. This high-powered pavement scorcher was manufactured only in hardtop coupe form, but that doesn't limit its high desirability with today's enthusiasts and collectors.

The engine is 341 CID and capable of 320 horses. The new car buyer could get one for $3,683. It will cost you about twice that for one in "like-new" condition. The good news is, a year or two from now, it will cost the next guy a lot more to buy it from you.

Fig. 4-9. The 1955 DeSoto Fireflite.

Fig. 4-10. In 1956, DeSoto Fireflite paced the 500 at Indianapolis.

In 1957, DeSoto made the Adventurer a sub-series of the Fireflite (in 1958 it would be a separate series again) and introduced the convertible as a stablemate to the hardtop. Sitting again on a 126-inch wheelbase, the convertible weighs in at 4,235 pounds; aboout 200 more than the hardtop.

A popular option on the Adventurer in 1957 was dual headlights and nearly all Adventurers were equipped with them new. However, because they were an option, you may run into a few '57 Adventurers that aren't so equipped. As with any other option, the car with is worth more than the one without.

The hot DeSoto engine for 1957 models is the 345 cubic inch, 345 horsepower unit mounted with dual four-barrel carbs. Torque-Flite and power brakes were standard in '57. I don't know anyone who ever buried the needle on the 150 mph speedometer, but I can say that the car is fast. It'll do 60 from a dead stop in about 7.5 seconds.

Fig. 4-11A&B. Of all DeSotos, the powerful Adventurers of 1956-59 are the most sought after. Here's the '59 version coming and going.

The original selling price for an Adventurer in 1957 was around $4,200.

A minor facelift was part of the new DeSoto in 1958; dual headlights became standard. The price of a new Adventurer jumped about $150 in 1958, but it was still cheaper than the Chrysler 300D. And you really didn't get less car by buying a DeSoto as some Chrysler fans will tell you.

The standard engine here is a 361 cube number that puts out 345 horsepower. If you're lucky enough to find one of the very few equipped with optional fuel injection, you get 10 nasty horses more.

In 1958, as DeSoto celebrated its 30th birthday with the production of a truly superb automobile in the Adventurer, the sagging economy of the nation grew into a full-fledged disaster. Everybody suffered that year, especially the automobile manufacturers. Especially DeSoto.

The 1959 DeSoto sure doesn't provide any hints that the company was sinking fast. The Adventurers of '59 look pretty much like those of '58; maybe a little better (Fig. 4-11). The engine is just as powerful, minus fuel injection. Road handling qualities are perhaps a little better. The list of options available in 1959 was longer than Abe Lincoln's arm. The 1959 DeSoto is everything it can and should be.

DeSotos are fairly popular with enthusiasts and collectors now, but in 1959 they weren't very popular with new car buyers. Sales were better than in '58, but fate was playing its part. DeSoto's days were numbered.

The last DeSoto was a 1961. It came off the assembly line in December 1960. The adventure was over.

DODGE

In 1953 Dodge automobiles finally started looking and performing like the Fifties cars rather than fugitives from the Forties. Along with the restyling came the Red Ram V-8, 241 cubes delivering 140 horsepower. In fact, the Red Ram is a miniature Hemi. It delivers an ideal combination to those who possess it now; it performs well and economically. To top that off, it's nearly fault free.

The first really hot Fifties Dodge is the 1954 Dodge Royal 500 convertible and you have a true to life, head turning dreamboat. In my opinion, it is the best looking and best all-around Dodge of the decade (Fig. 4-12).

Fig. 4-12. Dodge led the way around the Indy oval in 1954. That's Jerry Lewis and Dean Martin aboard.

Styling changes from '53 are minute. Base V-8 is the 241 cuber, putting out 150 horses. A PowerFlite automatic could be had optionally on 1954 Dodges. The Royal convertible is of itself a very snappy looking automobile, but when coupled with the 500 package, commemmorating Dodge's Indy 500 pacer of that year, look out! The 500 option put the new car buyer out something like $3,000. What the fellow got for his cash was special Pace Car trim, a continental kit, Kelsey Hayes wire wheels and a special version of the Red Ram with race-ready, four-barrel carburetion. If you can't find a 500, lay hands on a regular Royal and start adding your own options. You might not end up with a 500, but you will end up with one attention attracting machine.

When 1955 rolled around, Dodge, like everything else in the Chrysler Corporation family, was adorned with Exner's new body style. Depending on which Dodge you choose, it comes with or without small add-on chrome fins. All 1955 Dodges are mounted on a 120-inch wheelbase.

The pick of the litter is the Dodge Custom Royal Lancer with a wild three-tone paint scheme and those little chrome fins I just mentioned (Fig. 4-13). Other chrome trim can be found around headlights, on the hood and down across the beltline, around all windows, along the rocker panels and, of course, in taillight, bumpers and grille.

Engine choices begin with a 270 cubic inch V-8 that produces 183 horsepower at 4400 rpm. The optional Power Pac would give you an extra 10 horses from the same block with a four-barrel carb and dual exhausts. The standard transmission is a three-speed manual. Overdrive is a desirable option to have on this car as well as the dash mounted PowerFlite automatic.

One other '55 Dodge that should be mentioned in passing is the bizarre Custom Royal LaFemme. New, it came with rain cape, umbrella, boots and purse; all in matching colors, of course. If you haven't guessed, the LaFemme was intended as the "she" version of a "he" car. The best that can be said of this special model is that it is interesting.

In 1956, Dodge entered the space age with real tailfins push button automatic transmission and the powerful D500 engine option. D500 stands for 315 cubic inches and 260 horsepower with dual quad pots for carburetion. Top speed with this setup is around 135 miles per hour. Again, Custom Royals are the hot number with the automotive fraternity.

Dodge styling was completely redone in 1957. The result is a group of large, chromed and finned brutes that look as if they would

Fig. 4-13. 1955 Dodge Royal Lancer.

have no problem ruling the highway. Dodge called its finned look Autodynamic and used words like tornado and hurricane to describe performance. With Hemis available from 325 cube/245 horse to 354 cube/340 horse versions, high performance is definitely a part of the 1957 Dodge vocabulary.

Look for a Custom Royal again. The more powerful the engine option the better. Standard transmission models are a little quicker, but the push button automatic is no poke. All cars with the big engine (D500) option were orginally equipped with a heavy duty suspension package including torsion bars, stiffer springs and heavy duty shocks.

For 1958 and '59, Dodge Custom Royal remained basically the same car as the 1957. Instead of being powered by a Hemi, they are powered by a Wedge. They ride the same 122-inch wheelbase. The most desirable engine option for the decade's last Dodges comes in the form of fuel injection in 1958 models. The option didn't sell well back in '58, but it is pretty dependable and will add a number of greenbacks to the value of a Fifties Dodge (Fig. 4-14).

IMPERIAL

As of 1955 (and until the mid-Seventies), Imperial became an individual make in the Chrysler Corporation stable. And when the first one rolled off the line, it was perfectly clear that Chrysler had a real luxury barge on its hands. From the divided egg crate grilles up front, to the sparrow strainer taillights at the rear, the 1955 Imperial is a dreamboat in the most elegant sense (Fig. 4-15).

These cars are chrome heavy front and rear, while maintaining very clean side lines. The powerplant is a 331 cube Hemi worthy of 250 horses. Interiors are comparable to those of the Cadillacs and Continentals of the same period. Performance wise, they are better than either, and cost wise, they are cheaper.

In 1956, the Imperial grew fins like the other Chrysler products with sparrow strainer taillights, retained from the '55 Imperial perched on top. The shortest wheelbase on a '56 Imperial is 133 inches, three inches longer than the '55's (Fig. 4-16).

In addition to the standard Imperials, there are the more formal Crown Imperial limousines and sedans. These cars are big, impressive and good looking, but they entirely lack the excitement inherent in the design of their less ostentatious brothers.

The fins became huge sweeping things in 1957, so huge that the distinctive taillights were moved from atop to within the fin. The best of the breed, at least from my point of view, is the super luxurious Imperial Crown convertible. The power to make this brute perform is provided by a 392 cube, 325 horse Hemi.

By now, you're tired of hearing it, but like all the other Chrysler Corporation products, the only really big change for 1958-59 is the switch to a Wedge head engine.

Roughly 100,000 Imperials were produced from 1955-59. Every one of them would bring a premium today. If you want one,

Fig. 4-14. A 1959 Dodge in attendance at one of the hundreds of car shows carried on each summer.

Fig. 4-15. Imperial by Chrysler, circa 1955.

Fig. 4-16. 1956 Imperial ads said, "The man who drives the Imperial . . . sees the future taking shape."

Fig. 4-17. Shown together are the 1958 Plymouth Fury and 1956 DeSoto Golden Adventurer. Both were based on the Chrysler 300.

Fig. 4-18. Plymouth Fury for 1958.

and can afford it, try to get either a convertible or one of the very rare Crown Imperial limousines designed and built in Turin, Italy by Ghia, beginning in 1957.

PLYMOUTH

Spending a lot of time on a chapter about Plymouths in a book on dreamboats and milestones would be akin to giving you lessons in putting people to sleep. The word Plymouth rarely comes up in a conversation dealing with the kind of cars we are dealing with in this book.

In spite of their reputation as poor relations, though, the Plymouths of the Fifties are every bit the cars the rest of their Chrysler cousins are. Sure, there is nothing that comes quite up to the performance standards of the Chrysler 300 or DeSoto Adventurer. And there is nothing quite as luxurious as even the plainest Imperial. But, if we are going to discuss the Dodge Custom Royal, we can hardly ignore the 1956-59 Plymouth Fury Sport and Sport Fury (Fig. 4-17).

Actually, on a scale, the Fury would rank just above the Dodge Custom Royal and just below the DeSoto Adventurer. Remember, though, the distance between the performance of one Chrysler product and another during the horsepower race years is very small.

The Fury was introduced in 1956 as a limited edition hardtop with gold-anodized side trim. The Fury engine is a 303 cubic inch V-8 that puts out 240 horsepower at 4800 rpm. A four-barrel, dual exhausts and other hot items combine to make it capable of 60 mph in less than 10 seconds and a top speed of very near 140.

The Fury continued in production through 1959 with the same fin growths and engine changes as other Chrysler products. If you want a Fifties Plymouth, pick a Fury; if you want a Fury, pick a '56-58 (Fig. 4-18).

Chapter 5 American Motors

When I first started thinking about the various cars that could fit into this chapter, it seemed that there might be quite a few. But it wasn't long before the list was trimmed down to the 1951-54 Hudson Hornet and Nash-Healey that I'll get to shortly. Most cars were discounted very quickly because, in no way, shape or form, could they ever be considered either dreamboats or milestones. To be perfectly honest, in spite of all the fine workmanship that went into Hudsons, Nashes, Ramblers and Metropolitans during the years between 1949 and 1960, most of them just weren't capable of turning the heads of pedestrians or other drivers.

The last cars cut from my list were the infamous 1955-57 Hudsons and Nashes. The Hashes. The great unloved. I remember thinking back in 1959 what a dreamboat the '56 Hudson Hornet Hollywood was that my dad had just bought. It was splendid, with its continental kit and color scheme of white, red, black, gold and chrome. With front seats that folded down to meet the back, it was one of the great make-out machines of all time. I loved that car and I still love that car. The fact is, though, the car that seemed the ultimate dreamboat to me back then is considered by enthusiasts and collectors —when it is considered at all—as little more than a rather bizarre, and thankfully short-lived, curiosity.

With the Nashes removed from the list, I was left with a pair of pre-merger automobiles. I could have put them in separate chapters under separate headings of Hudson and Nash. I left them together under the American Motors banner because they were the seed of the company and the last truly individual examples of either make.

Let's dwell for a moment then on the greatest American stocker of the day and a sports car fit for competition at LeMans—the Hudson Hornet and the Nash-Healey.

HUDSON

The Hudson Hornet, like the Chrysler 300 and the 1955 Chevy, is a legend. A full-blown, bigger than life, quicker (at least in its day) than just about anything, legend. Unlike the 300 or the Chev, when the Hornet was introduced in 1951, it didn't look like some great new machine. The difference that made it more special than earlier Hudsons aren't even all that noticeable. Shucks, it looks pretty much like just another Hudson.

Let's begin at that point. First of all, there isn't anything wrong with looking like other Hudsons. One criticism is that the step-down design with Monobilt construction was produced for too long. By the time the Hornet came around, it was already an old design. It may have been old for Hudson, but it was still a few years ahead of the rest of the industry. In 1954, as Hudson was about to pass from the American scene, the rest of the automobile manufacturers had just caught up. If Hudson had survived without Nash into 1955, it probably would have been left in the dust design wise (it would be 1956 before Hudson was completely but of the performance picture).

When the Hornet came on the scene in 1951, it came with a totally reworked L-head engine (Fig. 5-1). This six cylinder mill measures 308 cubic inches and puts out 145 horsepower at 3800 rpm. It has a high compression aluminum head. That's just for beginners. Thanks to the wizardry of mechanics and racers like Marshall Teague, many Hornets were produced with a variety of performance options. AAA and NASCAR race rules from those days are no easier to understand now than they were then, but basically what they said was that to race it, it had to be available to the American public. Some of the goodies John Q. could get for his '51 Hornet included a hot cam, larger valves, overbored cylinders, headers and Twin H-Power. Twin H-Power consists of a dual induction manifold with twin carbs. A nifty set-up topped off by big red aircleaners with Twin H-Power spelled out in yellow (Fig. 5-2). Neat! Then of course there are also the usual suspension beefing bits and pieces. All of these things turn up on a surprising

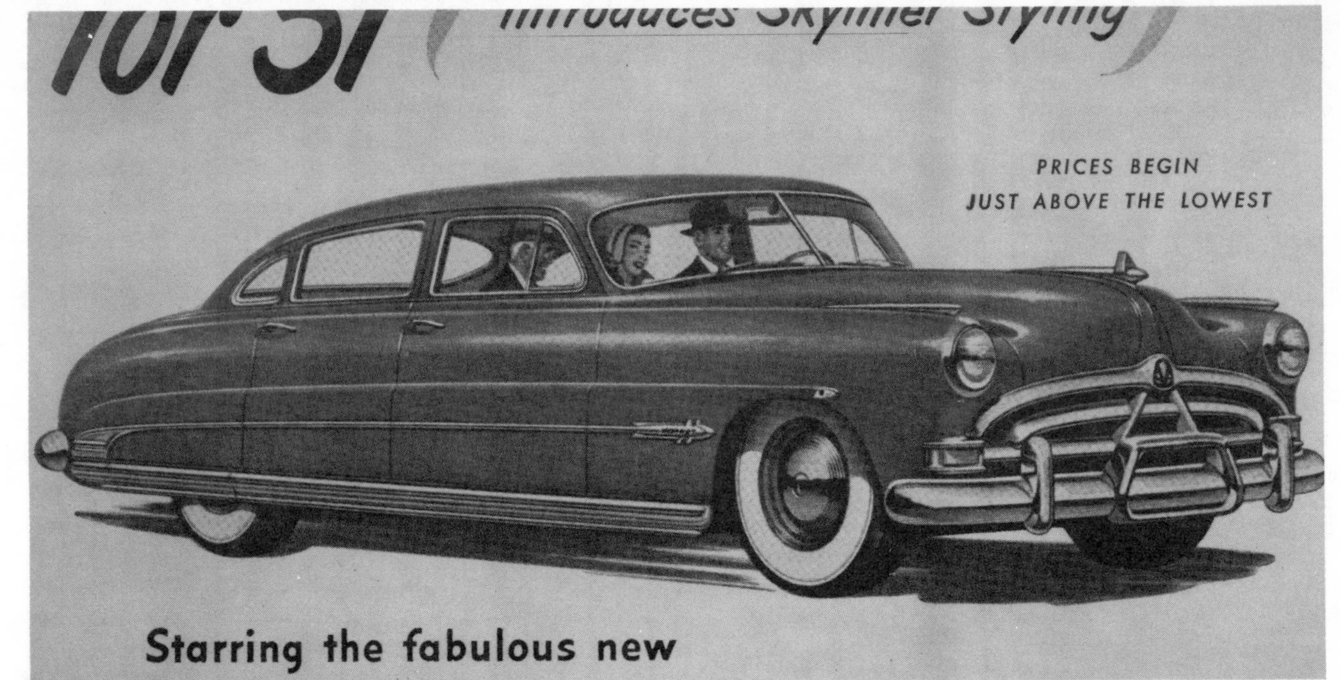

Fig. 5-1. The 1951 Hudson Hornet. Though not usually considered as such, it too was an early muscle car of sorts. What the mighty H-Power six gave away in size, it made up in torque.

Fig. 5-2. Artist Bruce Bingham considers the 1951 Hudson in one of his well-known cartoons.

Fig. 5-3. A 1952 Hudson Hornet.

number of Hornets today. What you may end up with is a Hornet powered by some 200 horsepower and capable of around 110 mph.

The look of the '51 Hornet is long, low and wide. Wheelbase is 124 inches. The look is pretty much the same as it was from 1948-50, and remained basically the same for '52 and '53, with an only slightly updated appearance in 1954.

A three-speed manual is the standard transmission on '51-'54 Hudsons. Overdrive and Hydra Matic were optional (Fig. 5-3).

In 1954, Hudson Hornet was built on the same wheelbase, with the same lists of standard equipment and options as in previous years. The base engine was still a 308 cuber, but minimum horsepower grew to 160. The more performance goodies, the higher your horsepower will be; just adding Twin H gives you 10 extra horses (Fig. 5-4). If you didn't already get the message, things were getting pretty stale at Hudson by mid-decade. If you go out and buy a 1954 Hornet, you are going to get an excellent automobile. Problem in '54 was that no matter how good it was, Hudsons were old hat (Fig. 5-5).

A last ditch effort to produce a new and different Hudson was made under the name Italia. Some 25 Italias were produced. They were small, futuristic Hudson sports cars. (If you find one today, it's worth a mint.) They were a failure.

On May 1, 1954, Hudson Motor Company died. On April 22, 1954, Hudson and Nash merged to form American Motors. On October 29, 1954, the last real Hudson left the assembly line.

Fig. 5-4. For the Hudson owner interested in power plus, Twin H-Power is the only answer.

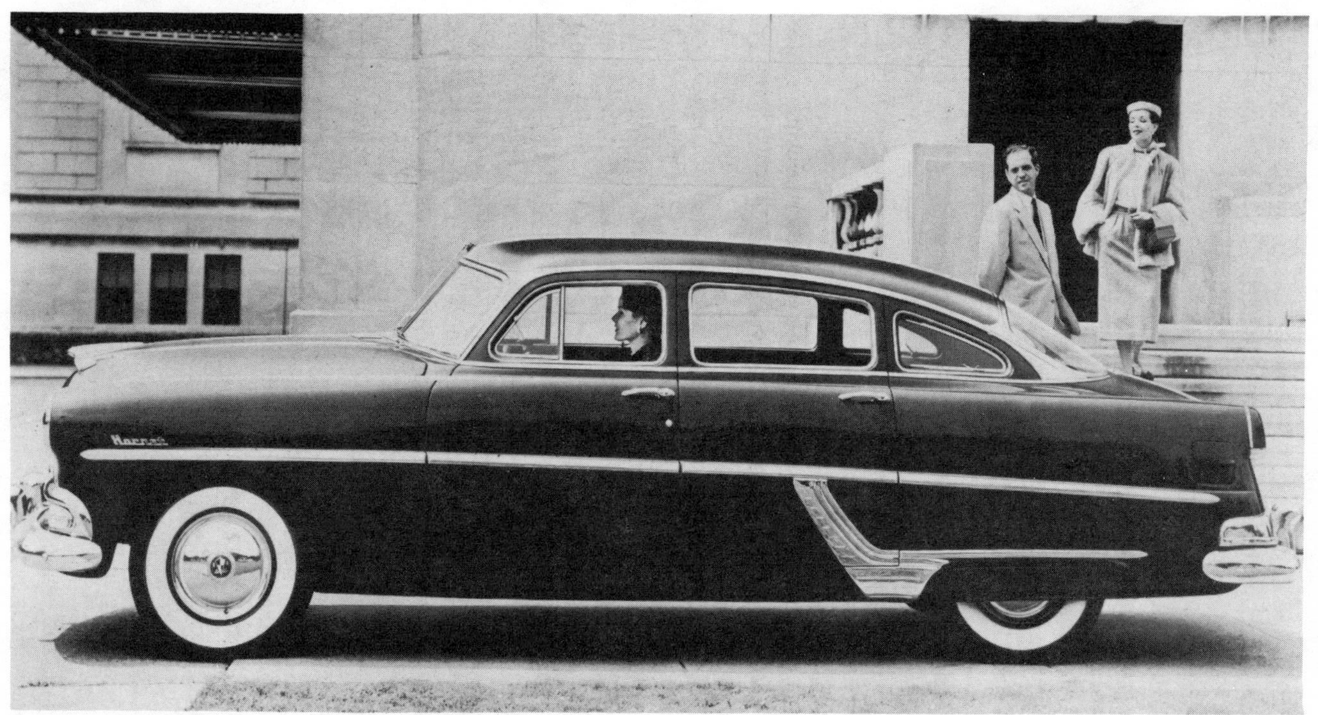

Fig. 5-5. In 1954, the last real Hudsons were produced. The models of '55-57 were more of a Hudson/Nash hash.

NASH-HEALEY

It's a damn shame that one of the finest sporting automobiles ever to be sold on the shores of the good old United States never had the chance to mature. The Nash-Healey is every bit the car the early Corvettes and Thunderbirds are—more in a lot of ways. It was ten times closer to being a sports car than anything that came before or immediately after it. Nash and American Motors didn't give it a chance. And with a total of just over 500 produced in four years, it's very clear that the American car buying public sure as hell never gave it a chance.

For the contemporary enthusiast or collector in search of a fine sports car, the Nash-Healey is the answer to a wealth of dreams. It's good looking, production was limited, yet more than half of those made are known to exist today, parts are available at a reasonable price, it drives great, it's sturdy and it is cheap. For some mysterious, but incredible, reason, the value of Nash-Healeys has not risen in the marketplace as did the value of the early Birds and Vettes. If you want one, get it now before everyone catches on (Fig. 5-6).

Before I get too carried away, let's take a look at some of the details. The idea for the Nash-Healey was born in 1949, when Nash President, George Mason, and sports car racer/builder Donald Healey met on an ocean voyage from England to the States. When they walked off the ship, it was as partners agreed to build a new Nash-powered sports car. (It has been suggested that Healey got on the boat because he knew Mason was going to be there.)

The first Nash-Healey appeared in the autumn of 1950 as a 1951 model. Power is provided by a 234 CID, 125 horsepower Nash six. Transmission is three-speed manual with overdrive. The car weighs 2,690 pounds and is 170 inches long, mounted on a short, 102-inch wheelbase. Price was $4,063 off the dealership floor.

The first Nash-Healeys look a great deal like a cross between a Jaguar and an early Austin-Healey with Nash trim. The only flaw in this design is an ugly chrome air scoop. The main identifying characteristic—other than the Nash-Healey script on the upper portion of the front fenders—is the Nash grille set nicely into Healey's design. Bumpers are also Nash. Only 104 1951 Nash-Healeys were built.

In 1952, the Nash-Healey was redesigned by Pinin Farina who also did the rest of the Nash line. The basic shape of the body is more bulbous up front, slightly squared-off in back. Small reversed

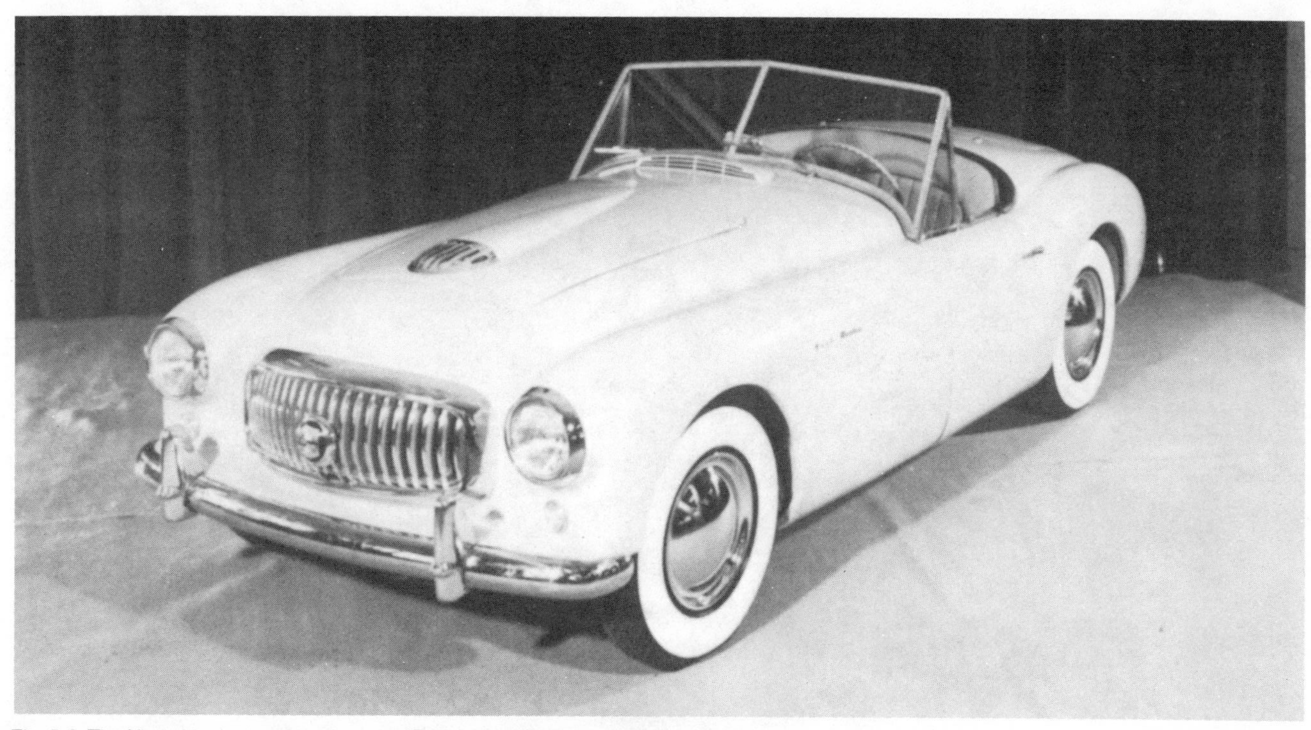

Fig. 5-6. The Nash-Healey, an American and British hybrid, burst upon the scene.

Fig. 5-7. The second series Nash-Healeys were designed by the Italian Pinin Farina. Shown is a 1953 model.

Fig. 5-8. The last Nash-Healey made the scene in 1955. The only real updating was in the area of the hardtop.

tailfins resembling air scoops are mounted toward the back of the rear fenders. The ugly hoodscoop is replaced by a cleaner, stock Nash design. Headlights are moved inboard from the fenders to the new Nash grille, creating the one big design flaw in that model. The two-piece windshield is replaced by a one-piece curved affair. A Pinin Farina/Nash insignia on the lower portion of the front fenders takes the place of Nash-Healey script of the '51's.

Early 1952 Nash-Healeys carry the same engine as the '51 models. Later '52's come equipped with a 252 cube mill that develops 135 horsepower at 4000 rpm. A pair of Carter carbs replace the dual SU's of '51.

The 1951 Nash-Healeys have steel bodies. Models of '52 and later are aluminum. Both have advantages and disadvantages —mainly, steel rusts and aluminum bends.

When 1953 made its appearance, the Nash-Healey roadster remained basically the same (Fig. 5-7). The new model for that year was the LeMans hardtop. The LeMans sits on a 108-inch wheelbase and measures a total of 181 inches. Weight is just short of 3,000 pounds, about 300 more than the roadster. There is a rear passenger seat, but it's strictly a Munchkinland unit.

There are five more horsepower in the '53 Healey than in its elder kin. Transmission remains the same. (Why change a good thing?)

The only change in the 1954 Nash-Healey came in the form of a revised rear window for the hardtop. Only 90 Nash-Healeys were built in 1954 (Fig. 5-8).

It's questionable whether or not the Nash-Healey could have kept up with the competition if it had survived. For my money, Nash should have hung their hat on it and said to hell with the dogs they did go on to produce. Or maybe when Nash and Hudson merged...

Chapter 6 Packard And Studebaker

With Packards and Studebakers, we have a situation similar to that of Hudson and Nash. For a long time both were proud, independent makes, highly respected for their individual attributes. Unlike Hudson and Nash, Packard and Studebaker were unable to draw a breath of survival out of their unstable union. For Packard, the struggle ended in 1958 with the death of what could only be considered one of the great grotesques. If ever an automobile was driven to suicide by its sheer ugliness, the 1958 Packard was. But the company waited too long, there was no dignity in the passing. And Studebaker went out gasping for air in a world of heavy breathers.

Both Packard and Studebaker had long histories of building strong, dependable cars. In spite of the fact that some rather bizarre looking automobiles were produced, the tradition for quality continued right up the the very end. Why they couldn't make it, especially after the merger of the two companies, is anybody's guess. Whatever the underlying reasons for their failure were, it all boils down to one thing: Packard and Studebaker could not compete.

What remains of the two companies is a bunch of very popular enthusiast-type cars. Among them, a fair share are of the dream-boat and milestone breed. One of them even paced at Indy. Let's take a look at the top of the line.

PACKARD

Packard entered the fab Fifties wearing what even Packard execs described as the "pregnant look." I gather this was not intended as a compliment. Personally, I don't think the 1950 Packards look all that bad. Sure, they're a little ungainly, especially in sedan form, but drop the top, and look out! Now you've got yourself a real live dreamboat.

As the ideal choice, take the 1950 Custom Eight convertible victoria. Sitting on its 127-inch wheelbase with its 356 cubic inch eight pounding out 160 horses, it is a thing to behold. The 1950 new Packard buyer also got an Ultramatic automatic transmission as standard equipment (Fig. 6-1).

For the guy that comes into possession of a '50 Packard now, there are some pleasant times ahead. These are some very nicely

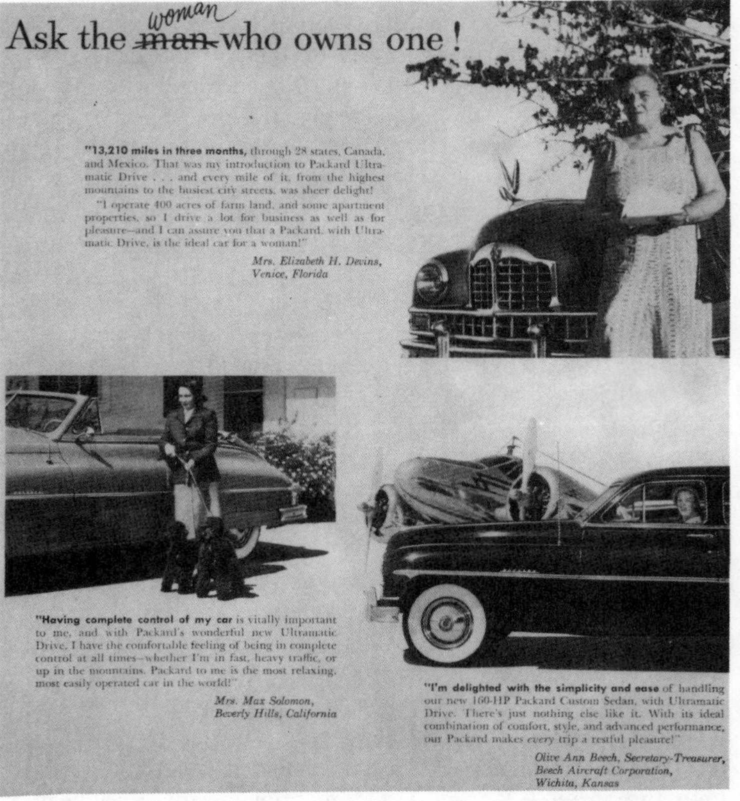

Fig. 6-1. In 1950, Packard changed their ad slogan to read, "Ask the woman who owns one."

engineered machines. If you come upon one in fine tune, you can expect it to stay that way without much trouble.

In 1951, Packard entered the new age with a completely restyled product. It also dreamt up a bunch of new names for its various models, including the 400 Patrician. This is the baby to have.

The Patrician sits on a wheelbase of 127 inches. The new 327 cube flathead engine came with 150 horses. All came equipped with Ultramatic. The shape is boxy, but with slightly rounded edges. Chrome is used extensively for a car produced this early in the decade. Bumper/grille is big and heavy with chrome, there's a side spear, three chrome whatzits on the rear fenders, splash guard, and trim strip at the lower half of those fenders. Get the message? These dreamboats are definitely not for the bashful.

Another Packard produced in 1951 that has become quite popular with the contemporary automobilist, is the 122-inch wheelbase 250. To many enthusiasts, the 250 convertible is the best looking pre-1953 Packard of all. It is equipped with the same 327 as the Patrician, so you can imagine the kind of performance it delivered. A three-speed manual transmission is standard equipment. If you bought one new, overdrive or an Ultramatic would cost you extra. In 1951, the three-speed turned out to be pretty popular on the 250, so be prepared to shift for yourself if you want one.

The 1952 Packards are, with only a couple exceptions, identical to the '51's. The only exterior difference between the two is that the Packard Pelican got his wings pinned back. Beyond that, Ultramatic was updated and Easamatic power brakes became available (Fig. 6-2). A car with either or both of these will, of course, command a premium of the hobby car shopper. You know how it is with options, they are those bothersome things (on all cars) that constantly broke down when the cars were new, but which cost an arm and a leg now.

In 1953, the prettiest postwar Packard of all joined the flock. Today, it will send enthusiasts and collectors stark raving bananas, just like the Buick Skylark, Cadillac Eldorado and Olds Fiesta of the same year. Next time you're in a crowd of postwar car people, just mention the name Caribbean and a few of the folks are guaranteed to start salivating all over themselves.

Why not? The 1953 Packard Caribbean is beautiful (Fig. 6-3). Like the three GM cars I just mentioned, the Caribbean is possessed of those elusive qualities that make a car a landmark the

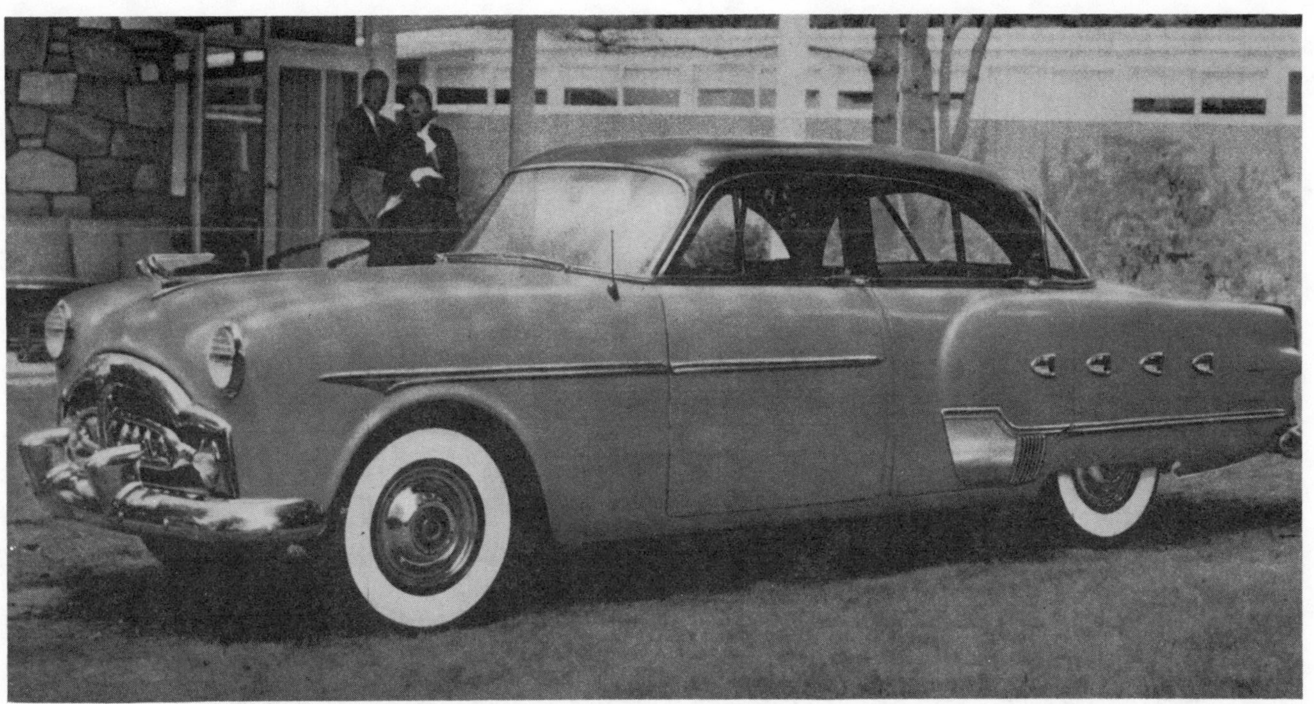

Fig. 6-2. 1952 Packards were "fashion keyed" by Dorothy Draper, whoever she was.

minute it rolls off the line. Visually, it is pretty much the same shape as its immediate predecessors. The biggest difference is that the chrome treatment is a lot more dignified than in previous years. In fact, the sides are almost totally free of chrome. The look is terrific.

Power for the '53 Carribean is provided by the 327 cuber, now beefed up to 180 horses. Standard tranny is the three-speed. However, if you were a highroller back in 1953, you could start with your basic Caribbean, then begin tacking on the extra dollar goodies like overdrive or an automatic trans, power brakes, power steering, power seats, power windows, radio with electric antenna and speaker, and so on, and so on. Wire wheels are a standard item.

Only 750 Caribbeans were built in '53, so if you want one, plan on taking a while to find it and paying through the proverbial nose when you do. If you're lucky, you might find one for $11,000 or thereabouts. Several automotive journalists have referred to the 1953 Caribbeans as limited edition dream cars. It is the perfect description.

While 1953 models are among the most sought after of all postwar Packards, putting your paws on a '54 will provide you with nearly the same thing. Only a couple of almost unnoticeable changes help tell the two years apart. Back-up lights are built into the taillight assembly and the headlights on the '54's are encased in deep dish rims with small chrome apertures top and center.

The Caribbeans produced in 1954 carry a chrome trim strip across the rear fender, emphasized by two-toning. Otherwise, the Caribbeans are pretty much the same cars as those produced in 1953. They are hardly the bastards some automotive writers have made them out to be.

The big news for Packard in 1954 was its merger with the struggling Studebaker. It's ironic that of the two combined companies, Packard bit the dust first, and Studebaker was, temporarily, the survivor. After all, it was Packard money that brought the two together in 1954; all of which hardly matters now. The Packard look continued through 1955 and 1956 before becoming a grotesque combination of the two makes, culminating in one of the ugliest automobiles ever to roll on rubber, the Packard Hawk. This is a car with no redeeming social characteristics. No more need be said of it. But what about the Packards of 1955 and '56?

When the 1955 Packard line debuted, it was in new clothes and with some other pretty interesting developments, too. Rather than

Fig. 6-3. The Packard Caribbean appeared in 1953, the same year as GM's production dream cars; Skylark, Eldorado and Fiesta. Today, it is just as highly prized.

being totally unique from the earlier Packards, the '55's are a refinement of the existing design. The problem is that using the word "refinement" implies that the look of the Packard of 1955 is superior to that of 1954. This is definitely not the case (Fig. 6-4). Rather, the 1955 Packard displays all the signs of the next illogical step into the era of chrome and fins. The sides take on a greater sweep, ending in fenders with a distinct finned look, even though there aren't really any fins. Multiple chrome strips and two (and three) toning announce Packard's servitude to the shiny god. The headlights peer out from under great heavy brows of steel and chrome. The grille that is distinctly Packard on '54 and earlier models is an egg crate copycat on the '55's. The overall look, rather than being ugly, is that of a dreamboat from bumper-to-bumper and road-to-roof. And with a real wraparound windshield to boot (Figs 6-5 and 6-6).

Naturally, the Caribbean is once again the cream of the crop. Whatever the 1955 Packard is, the 1955 Packard Caribbean is more. The Caribbean isn't the only '55 popular with collectors now. The Four Hundred and the Clipper Custom don't come near the Caribbean, but they are still highly sought-after collector and enthusiast cars.

A number of changes and improvements show up on the 1955 Packards. The biggest of them is Torsion Level suspension. The system keeps all four corners of the Packard level at all times

Fig. 6-4. Packard's 1955 Caribbean convertible.

Fig. 6-5. The cockpit like dash of the 1955 Packard 400.

through the use of extra long torsion bars connecting front and rear wheels with an automatic height control. I can't say just how dependable the Torsion Level suspension is—though I'm told it's very dependable—but having seen it work on several occasions, I can say that it looks impressive as hell (Fig. 6-7).

Besides their milestone suspensions, the '55 Packards are powered by new and improved V-8 engines. The outdated straight eight was replaced once and for all during the same year Chevrolet performed the small block miracle. Displacement on 1955 Packard mills ranges from 320 all the way to 352 cubic inches. Horsepower starts at 225 and ends with a max of 275 in the four-barrel mounted Caribbeans.

Fig. 6-6. Packard 400 for 1955.

The 1955 Clipper sits on a 122-inch wheelbase. The Four Hundred and the Caribbean both rest on 127-inch wheel bases.

One thing that must be mentioned about the Packards of 1955 is that they have a very bad reputation for dependability. One collector tells me he loves his '55 Packard so much because he loves to work on cars and, with the Packard, there is always something to work on. Other owners say it's all bad rap. All I can say is that the reputation is an old one that seems to hold true in some cases. How's that for being vague?

The 1956 Packards, like the '54 Hudsons, are the last of the real thing. While they are hardly "the greatest Packards ever," as contemporary ads would have you believe, they are equally as interesting as the '55's and, in some ways, better cars.

Appearance-wise, the '56 Packards differ very little from the '55's. Only the most inconsequential changes have been made in trim and lighting. Just enough so that in 1956, Packard execs could tell the new cars from the old ones. It's a silly game, but automobile manufacturers, not generally being possessed of great intellect, have played it for years. They think they are putting something over on the new car buying public: the public shrugs its shoulders and lets it go.

Unfortunately for Packard in 1956, the public wasn't letting anything go. The bad reputation of the '55's had already gotten around and hordes of buyers were staying away. To some extent, this all pays off very nicely for the fellow who wants to buy a mid-Fifties Packard now. By buying a '56, rather than a '55, you will more than likely be able to get a better car for less money.

In addition to Torsion Level suspension being made standard equipment on 1956 models, all came with push button Ultramatic transmissions (much improved over the '55's) and limited slip rear ends. Engines range from 352 to 374 in cubes and from 240 horsepower to a manifold melting 310 in (what else?) the Caribbean.

Sure, Packard built cars in 1957 and '58, but as I said before, they really aren't worth considering. Packard, like Hudson before it, began the decade as a proud independent. At some point near the decade's center though, all of the pride vanished. All that was left was a name.

STUDEBAKER

There are a very few cars that when mentioned in conversation will immediately summon up visions of the Fifties to the

Fig. 6-7A & B. These photos illustrate one of many 1955 Packard options, Torsion Level Ride.

enthusiast and non-enthusiast alike. DeSoto is one. Kaiser is another. On a much more pronounced scale, Studebaker is most certainly one. Studebakers are continuing symbols of the garish Fifties on the highways of the Eighties. Why? Who really knows. Beginning in 1952, Studebaker produced one Indy Pace Car, a couple of certified milestones and a bunch of dreamboats. Yet, when considered next to some of the most outstanding American automobiles of the Fifties, Studebakers seem flawed. So what is the answer to the phenomenal popularity of the Stude? I'm not sure. I do have a guess though. Magic. Yeah, that's right, magic. What else could it be?

Studebaker had big plans for 1952, its 100th year in the wheeled vehicle business. In those 100 years, the company, started by the Studebaker brothers, produced some seven million horse and engine powered vehicles. The plan was to introduce an all new and wonderful Studebaker for the big year. Unfortunately, the best laid plans oft go astray. It's hard to say what went astray for Studebaker as the 1952 models went into production, but the resulting car was obviously not all new and wonderful in all ways. That doesn't mean it wasn't an okay machine though.

First, the boys of Indy chose a 1952 Studebaker Commander Regal convertible to pace the May classic (Fig. 6-8). As everybody has guessed by this time, a car can be as ugly as sin and still be much sought after if it is chosen to pace. Well, the '52 Commander Regal is not ugly—in fact, it's better looking by far than the '51. That makes it all the more exciting. Just think how hot it would be now if Studebaker had been able to make the big redesign in time.

The Studebaker Commanders made in 1952 sit on a 115-inch wheelbase. A 232 cube V-8 puts out some 120 horsepower. A top speed of somewhere around 95 mph is possible with a highly tuned engine. A three-speed manual was 1952's standard tranny. For extra cost, the new car buyer could get overdrive or an automatic. Obviously, if you find a car that carries either of these options, it is going to be worth a little more. In fact, I can't stress heavily enough the value placed on options by enthusiasts and (especially) collectors. For instance, overdrive on a '52 Commander will add around $75. An automatic could be good for as much as $200. If your Commander carries all the options of a Pace Car replica, you can figure it's worth in the neighborhood of $2,000 more in excellent condition.

Remember those big changes Studebaker had planned for its first century models? Well, they appeared in 1953. In the same year that produced the Cadillac Eldorado, Buick Skylark, Olds Fiesta, Chevrolet Corvette and Packard Caribbean, Studebaker brought out the exciting Loewy coupes. Only 1955 can be considered a milestone year of equal standing in the history of the American automobile.

Fig. 6-8. A 1952 Commander convertible paced that year's Indy 500 with 1951 winner Lee Wallard and his family aboard.

Back to the 1953 Studebaker. As hinted in the previous paragraph, there are really only two cars— both certified milestones—to be considered; the Champion and Commander, Starlight and Starliner coupes, designed by Bob Bourke under the direction of Ray Loewy. Studebaker had been just a little ahead of its time since 1947. With these two new coupes, Studebaker shot straight ahead into the space age (Fig. 6-9).

Riding on their 120.5-inch wheelbases, the '53 Stude coupes are almost flawless. Function and form combine to produce the nearly perfectly designed (if not pretty) automobile. A fitting testimony to the aerodynamics of the coupes is made annually as examples still appear and make very respectable showings on the salt at Bonneville (Fig. 6-10).

Starlight and Starliner coupes can be found powered by both sixes and V-8's, with the eight being the most desirable of the two. The eight is a 120 horsepower job. The 169 cube six develops 85 horses. Overdrives and automatics are found on some surviving coupes as optional equipment. Power steering was also offered in 1953. A Borg-Warner mechanical power steering unit signifies that your car is an early '53 model. A hydraulic GM unit means it is a later car. Other options to look for in particular on these cars are the deluxe upholstery and the fine looking, but seldom seen, factory wire wheel covers.

Very little is different between 1953 and 1954 Starliner and Starlight coupes. In fact, about the only difference you will see are a pair of slightly larger bumper guards and an egg crate effect in the place of a single horizontal bar in the grille. In other words, if you

Fig. 6-9. The 1953 Loewy coupes drew attention from all quarters and deservedly so.

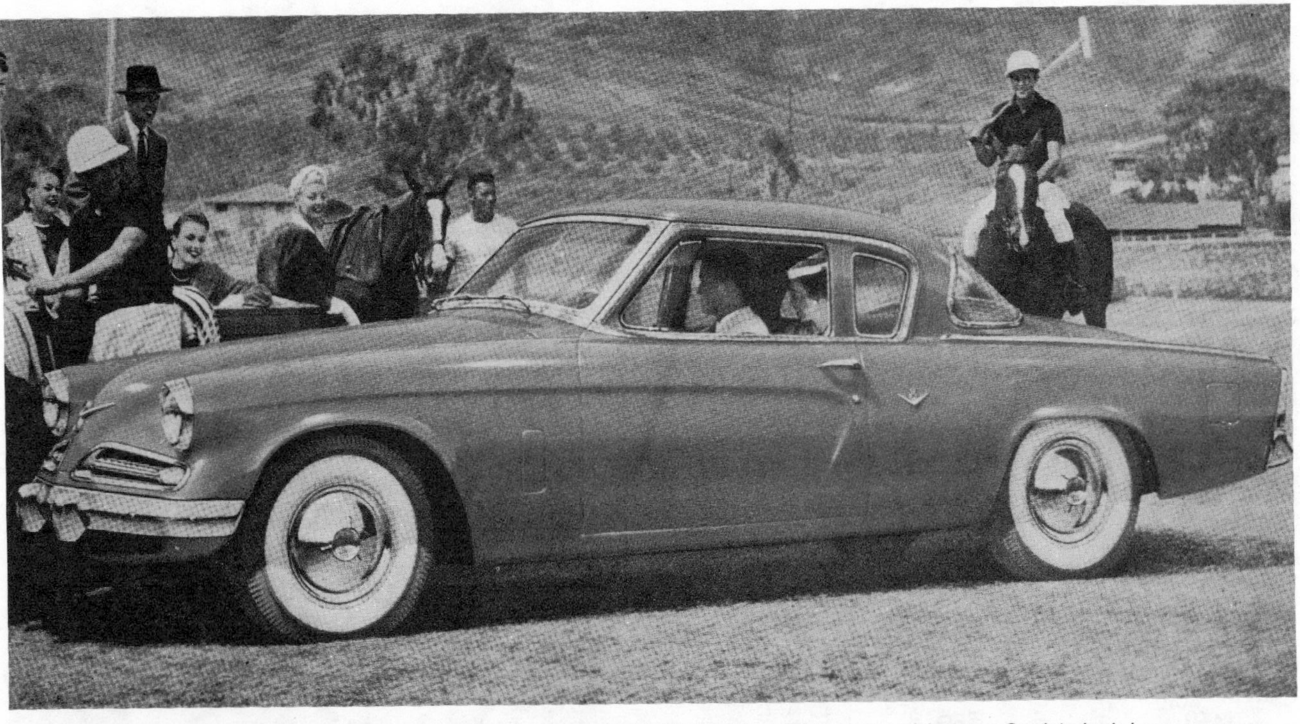

Fig. 6-10. The directors of New York's Fashion Academy presented their 1953 gold medal for style and design to Studebaker's Loewy coupes.

can't get a '53, settle for a '54 (Fig. 6-11). Some even like the '54's better.

And, before we move on to the '55's, yes, there is a way to tell a Starliner and Starlight apart. The Starliner is a hardtop, while the Starlight has a roof pillar.

The Studebakers of 1955 look much like those produced in 1953-54. The big difference is that the clean machine of earlier years became a dream machine decked out in chrome; lots of it. To say it is a little overdone is a gross understatement.

The hot bomb among the '55's is the top of the line President (a name last used by Studebaker in 1942) Speedster (Fig. 6-12). The Speedster was introduced midway through the model year as a five passenger coupe of the hardtop variety. The Speedster provides the enthusiast with sporty looks and performance plus room for the entire family. It's economical, too. This kind of car began to fade in the Sixties and disappeared entirely in the Seventies. Now, there are plenty of cars with equal and better mileage ratings. There are cars built to perform. There are cars that will carry a family of five. Unfortunately, all of these traits haven't been combined in one car for two decades. This is the kind of thing that makes so many Fifties cars, including Studebakers, the excellent bargains they are today.

Taking a look at the chrome vision that is a 1955 Studebaker President Speedster tells us a little about the very limited mentality of the people who make the decisions in the automobile industry. Just look at it, a plain yet attractive automobile. For some reason, it's not selling particularly well. "Well," says the Stude exec, "the boys o' the Big Three are addin' chrome. Why don't we add some chrome too?" So, instead of adding a little chrome, they slap it on everywhere. Just for good measure, they added two and three-tone paint jobs, including the ultimate combo of the decade, pink and black.

Fig. 6-11. A '53 Loewy coupe with '55 trim on hood and fenders.

Fig. 6-12. 1955 Studebaker President speedster.

Starting at the front of the car, the modest grille and bumper are replaced by a heavy chrome nose. Headlights are encircled by wide chrome rims. Shiny trim fins perch on top of both front fenders and at hood center. All windows are encircled by chrome. A widening trim spear trails along the entire side of the car from headlight to taillight. All that's missing are the fins.

The Speedster's wheelbase is 120 inches. Bumper to bumper, the Speedster measures 204 inches. Power is supplied to the rear wheels courtesy of Studebaker's Passmaster V-8. This 259 cubic inch mill puts out 185 horsepower at 4500 rpm. It is mounted with a four-barrel carb and dual exhausts. Bore and stroke is 3.56 x 3.25. Compression ratio is 8:1. It's likely that most Speedsters were fitted with automatics, but you might find one with three-speed or three-speed and overdrive.

The Speedster's interior is complemented by quilted leather and a special instrument panel. Also standard equipment are a 160 mph speedometer and tinted windshield. On the outside, you should see chrome extensions off the duals, backup lights, dual rearview mirrors mounted on the doors, fog lamps and factory wire wheel hubcaps.

In 1955, a brand new one would have cost you about $3,300. Today, you can get a like new one for around 10 .

It will surprise some other writers to hear me say it, but the '55 Speedster was not the last of Studebaker's dreamboats. In 1956, when Studebaker introduced its first Golden Hawk, the American public may not have rushed out to buy it, but you can bet that when one drove by, it got noticed. The same holds true of the Hawks today. They are guaranteed to draw wolf whistles and stares at the stoplight derby. It might be noted here, however, that Hawks are not the ideal pick-up cars. I remember how hard my friend and I tried to pick up girls in his '56 Studebaker Hawk, before we finally gave up and went home to get my '56 Olds. I think the whole thing had something to do with the sinister look of the car and how that reflected on the driver. Fortunately, most collector/enthusiast cars are not used for picking up girls.

While most of the Studebaker line for 1956 was completely redesigned, the Hawks were more or less just updates of the Loewy coupes. Updates, that is, with a definite trend away from sleek, toward gaudy.

Up front, the double Studebaker grille is retained from previous years. On the '56 Hawks, they are more like hollows than grilles. Between them sits a much larger squarish grille of chrome and wire mesh. A hood scoop appears just behind the grille. The biggest change in the look of the sporty Studebaker is the addition of a fin; it isn't a large fin, but no fin looks more out of place.

Looks aren't everything. The Golden Hawks have a reputation as performance road cars. The powerplant is a heavy 352 cubic inch Packard V-8 that produces 275 horses at 4600 rpm. A fourbarrel pot is mounted as the standard item. Handling, while not excellent, is very good. Many an enthusiast has been pleasantly surprised by his first drive in one of these machines. The only complaint one hears is that handling could be even better if the engine didn't make the front end overweight.

The return of the Studebaker engine, in the form of a 289 cuber, solved the overweight problem in 1957. Thanks to a McCulloch supercharger, the smaller Studebaker mill develops the same 275 horsepower as the gargantuan Packard. This kind of power from a small engine, plus fine handling, puts the 1957 Golden Hawk in a class near, if not with the '57 Thunderbirds and Corvettes. Room for four inside is a bonus. Problem is that the new car buying public wasn't ready for a high performance Studebaker in 1957. Somehow, the image of a Studebaker and the image of a performance car just wouldn't breed in the public eye.

While performance is improved on the '57 Studebaker, so is the body. The basic shape is the same, only on the '57's, one gets the feeling that the stylists had a specific idea in mind. When you look at a '56 Studebaker, you get the idea, or at least I do, that someone in the design studio was either very confused or very disturbed. The '57 Golden Hawk not only looks well thought out; it is, for my money, the best looking Studebaker since the 1953-54 Loewy coupes. Even the giant fins in contrasting color look right. The only thing that really looks out of place are the fender mounted parking lights up front, carried over from last year.

A great deal need not be said about the Studebakers of 1958 and '59. Again the Golden Hawk continues as the most collectible Studebaker of 1958. The Golden Hawk died the hard death, and in 1959, the Silver Hawk moved second banana to the number one slot.

During the last two years of the decade, Studebaker made few changes and little progress. The end was near in 1959. A quick look at the final Studebakers of the Fifties suggests that the end was even closer than it seemed. Today, enthusiasts and collectors are drawn to the final Hawks for their period look and fine performance. But among consumers of the late Fifties, the Hawk wouldn't fly.

Chapter 7
Kaiser-Frazer

Unlike Hudson, Nash, Studebaker and Packard, Kaiser-Frazer Corporation was not an old and respected independent that had somehow managed to survive WWII intact. Prior to the formation of the company, the name of Henry J. Kaiser was almost totally unknown in the automotive community. He had been involved in the building of highways, bridges, tunnels and ships, and saw a need for a lot of new automobiles on the happy day the war ended. At the start of the war, he set up the Henry J. Kaiser Company for the purpose of building those automobiles.

Joe Frazer, on the other hand, was quite well-known among the car folks. Starting out with a silver spoon firmly embedded in his mouth, he entered the automobile industry as a mechanic. He went on to found the first automotive technical school and organize the General Motors Acceptance Corporation. From there it was onward and upward, to and through Pierce, Maxwell, Chrysler, DeSoto and Willys-Overland. He named the Plymouth and the Jeep. It all culminated in the purchase of Graham-Paige in 1944. Good old Joe also had visions of peddling hundreds of thousands, maybe even millions of automobiles to the car-hungry, postwar public.

Inevitably, Kaiser and Frazer finally met and decided to share their dream in a more substantial way. During the summer of 1945 the two combined their assets. The Kaiser-Frazer Corporation became the offspring of the marriage of the Henry J. Kaiser

Company and Graham-Paige Motors. A former aircraft factory at Willow Run near Detroit was leased and Dutch Darrin was contracted to come up with a design for the new auto. Production begain in May 1946. It was the first Fifties-styled car.

FRAZER

There is considerably more to the early years of Kaiser-Frazer cars, but that is best handled in another book. Our interest in what became of the automotive marriage begins with the cars of 1950.

Specifically, we begin with only two Frazers: the certified milestone 1950 Frazer Manhattan and its successor of 1951.

To begin with, the 1950 Frazer is really a 1949 (Fig. 7-1). So, collectors who pay a premium because of the year on the title are getting ripped off. The Frazer's 123-inch wheelbase is based on a rigid X frame. The engine is a 226 cubic inch affair that puts out 112 horses with its six cylinders. The base price of some $3,000 included three-speed manual transmission, power top and windows on the convertibles, fender skirts, full wheel covers and wide whites. It is estimated that less than 50 of these convertibles were built and only a small percentage of those are likely to still exist. Obviously, if you end up owning one, it is an investment well worth hanging on to.

The body of the 1949-50 Frazer is bulbous, clean and aerodynamic in much the same way as the Hudsons, Lincolns and Mercuries of the same period. A modest use of chrome adds a touch of class, not crass.

The life span of the 1951 Frazer, including Manhattan models, is among the very shortest in automotive history (Fig. 7-2). The model year began in March, 1950 and ceased abruptly in August of the same year.

Fig. 7-1. Frazer Vagabond for 1949 and '50.

Dutch Darrin completely restyled the Frazers of '51. The cars have a stretched look compared to the previous models, even though they are built on the same 123-inch wheelbase. The front end has a charging look. Rear fenders are topped by some very fin-like bumps. The grille is a disaster not attractive in even the loosest sense of the word.

The powerplant in all 1951 Frazers is the old 226 cube six. Horsepower is up three to 115 and 3600 rpm.

Less than 11,000 1951 Frazers were built. Fewer than 150 of those were convertibles. Less than a third of those are likely to exist today. Frazer never even saw the beginning of calendar year 1951. By the time the clock struck 12 on Jan. 1, 1951, Frazer was just another memory. As went the car, so also went the man who gave it his name. In place of the car came the Henry J. In place of the man came Edgar Kaiser.

KAISER

The 1950 Kaisers look a lot like the 1950 Frazers (the more desirable of the two cars). You know what that means. That's right, the 1950 Kaisers, like brother Frazer, were the same as the 1949 models.

Among enthusiasts and collectors, the Vagabond and Virginian, both certified milestones, are the most popular 1950 Kaisers. Both cars ride a 123-inch wheelbase and are powered by 226 CID, 112 horsepower engines. Both are part of Kaiser's DeLuxe line.

The Virginian is the dreamboat of the two cars, but the Vagabond is by far the most interesting. The Vagabond is the predecessor of today's hatchback and kammback, multi-purpose cars. When they were new, the Vagabonds, as their name implies, were intended as go anywhere, do anything vehicles. The smart fellow is the guy who gets hold of one and uses it in the way it was first intended, while keeping it in fine tune. A passion for cars is becoming ever more expensive; the Vagabond is one of those cars that can do its part in helping to keep expenses down.

The Vagabond is simply a fancy version of the Kaiser Traveler. (Keep that fact in mind if you're willing to settle for a little less in your automobile.) Double rear doors open up and down to provide a station wagon-like cargo area. DeLuxe trim on the Vagabond includes fender skirts and full wheel covers. Wooden skid strips in the cargo area highlight the DeLuxe interior which also includes special cloths and vinyl. Roughly 4,500 Vagabonds were built and sold at just under $2,500 in 1949-50.

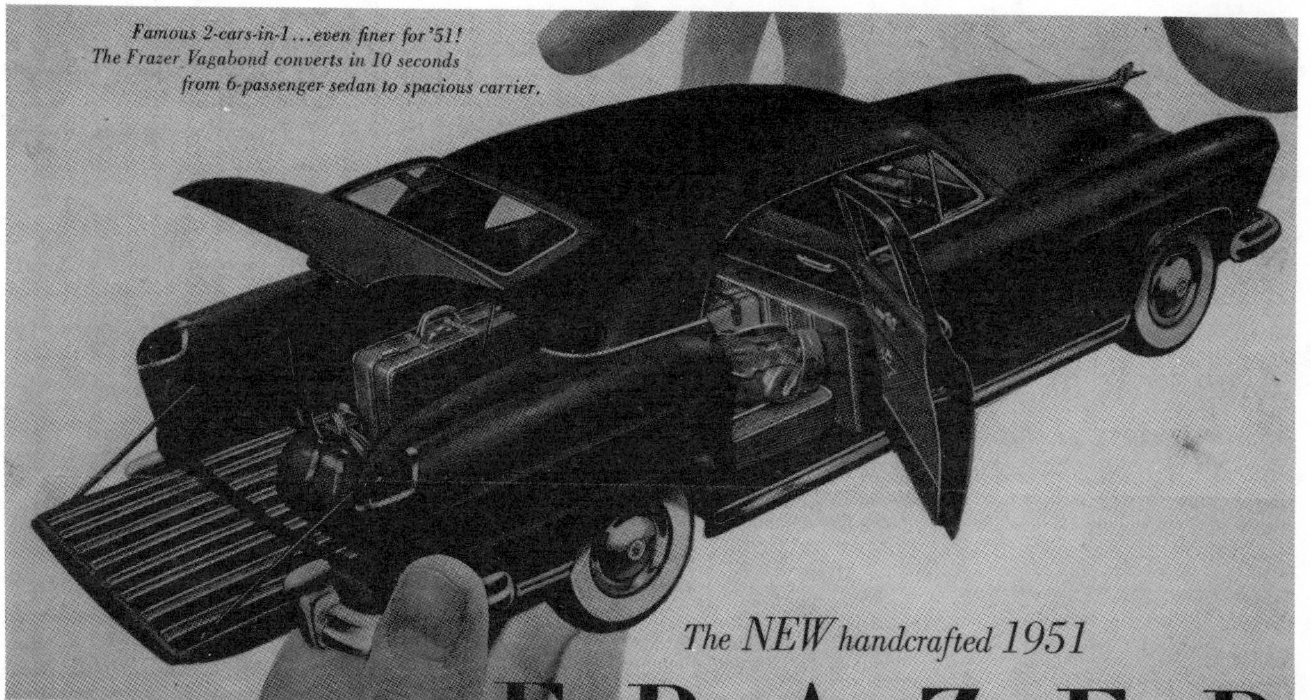

Famous 2-cars-in-1...even finer for '51!
The Frazer Vagabond converts in 10 seconds
from 6-passenger sedan to spacious carrier.
The NEW handcrafted 1951

Fig. 7-2. Six passenger sedan or utility vehicle? Take your choice with the 1951 Frazer Vagabond.

The 1949-50 Virginian reminds me of Ford's Crestliner of about the same period. Like the Crestliner, the Virginian was a car with a roof gimmick intended to compete with GM's new hardtops. Virginians have a standard steel roof jazzed up by a covering of nylon and the glass door post used on all Kaiser convertibles.

Kaiser-Frazer Corporation started out in business with the earliest introductions in the industry. This tradition continued with the 1951 Kaiser being introduced in February of 1950. And the intro was an exciting one. Bodywork is completely different from that of previous years. In fact, the Kaisers of 1951 are completely different from any other car of the same vintage. For the first time, Dutch Darrin was able to make a car look just the way he wanted. Thanks to the forward styling of hood and front fenders, the bubble-look roof and the Darrin dip (which occurs along the body line, about two-thirds back from the front of the car), the 1951 Kaisers look like they are in constant motion. The look fits its times, but if fits equally well on the road in the Eighties, which says a lot about the lasting power of good design. Again we return to the idea of function and form. When both criteria are met by the designer of an automobile, that automobile becomes timeless. The 1951 Kaiser comes very close.

The '51's sit on a 118-inch wheelbase and are pushed along by yet another version of the old flathead six, called Supersonic Six in 1951. Displacement is 226 cubes with a power rating of 115 horsepower. The standard transmission is a three-speed manual. A number of new car buyers opted for the addition of overdrive and still others chose the automatic (HydraMatic by General Motors).

Because they were the first of an exciting new body style, all '51 Kaisers rank high with enthusiasts and collectors. The milestone dreamboat DeLuxe and DeLuxe Virginians are near the top of everybody's list.

Another Kaiser, introduced in 1951, that gets consistently high marks from the car crowd is the Dragon. Four incarnations of the Dragon appeared in 1951; Golden Dragon, Silver Dragon, Emerald Dragon and Jade Dragon. All are based on the Kaiser DeLuxe series. In fact, at the risk of offending some owner who thinks they are more special, I'll go one step further by saying they are really little more than DeLuxe trim option packages. Basically all Dragons are pretty much alike, carrying as standard equipment, a number of things that were options on other models in 1951. Included in the Dragon package are extra plush carpeting, a vinyl roof (although some Dragons were made with only a contrasting color painted top), wide whitewall tires and HydraMatic. The various Dragons used different versions of the vinyl roof with different names; Dragon Vinyl, Dinosaur Vinyl and Tropical Vinyl. The Kaiser Dragon is a dear car, but when it comes to the fine points, a dragon is a dragon is a dragon.

The 1952 Kaisers were premiered to the public just prior to the first of the year; breaking the tradition of early introductions (Fig. 7-3). If the public was expecting a restyle for '52, and I doubt that they were, they didn't get it. After all, no company changed their cars completely every year. Kaiser made very little effort to update and improve their cars. Almost nothing is different from the '51 to the '52 Kaiser. The grille put on weight and the taillights changed shape. Big deal. Fortunately, the '51-'52 Kaisers have the kind of good looks that can survive without a lot of change.

In 1953, the Dragon moved closer to being a truly individual model. In a year that produced some of the most thrillingly attractive automobiles of all time, the Kaiser became just a bit boring. Except, that is, for the Dragon. When you look at a 1953 Kaiser Dragon, you are looking at one luxurious machine. I've used the words dreamboat and milestone over and over in this book. A lot of the cars we've looked at can be called both. The Dragon *is* one—in the extreme.

In addition to the vinyl hardtop—now called Bambu Vinyl—the Dragon is identifiable by script, name badges and its very own, extra long list of standard items. First off, the vinyl theme is carried to the inside of the car in the glove box, dash and door

Fig. 7-3. The 1952 Kaiser, with "the world's safest front seat." Or so the ads said anyway.

panels. Super plush carpets cover the floor in the passenger compartment and the trunk. Also included in the standard equipment list are HydraMatic, wide whites, special wheel covers, tinted glass, air conditioning and more, more, more. To top it all off, every 1953 buyer got his name engraved on a special dash plaque; a neat touch that can be played with by the guy who gets himself a Dragon now. Wheelbase on the '53 Kaisers is the same as 1952 models. So is the engine, although output is up to 118 horsepower.

By 1954, the handwriting was on the wall for Kaiser-Frazer Corporation. In fact, thanks to the phenomena that became such an important part of the automobile industry in the Fifties, the merger, it wasn't even K-F Corp. anymore. Instead, it was Kaiser-Willys. It was clear to all parties concerned that the final days were near.

What's amazing is that, in spite of the obvious facts, a pair of 1954 Kaisers are among the most collectibles Kaisers of all. One is the result of a fairly daring facelift. The other is the result of an act that was either very courageous, or very stupid, considering the state of the company.

First of these two cars is the 1954 Kaiser Manhattan (Fig. 7-4). It's basically the same car as it was in 1953 (when the name was revived), with some notable changes. Lots of chrome has been added. A hood scoop replaces the hood ornament. The rear window is a wraparound. The grille on the '54 Kaiser is one of the most unique ever to grace an American auto. It's a full width affair, made up of tightly spaced, concave grille bars. This is the kind of thing that put the nifty in the Fifties.

Another sweet addition to the Manhattan came along because the Kaiser company was unable to afford their own eight cylinder engine. What the Manhattan got (as an option) instead of an eight, was McCulloch supercharger. With it, the 226 six puts out a rowdy

Fig. 7-4. 1954 Kaiser Manhattan.

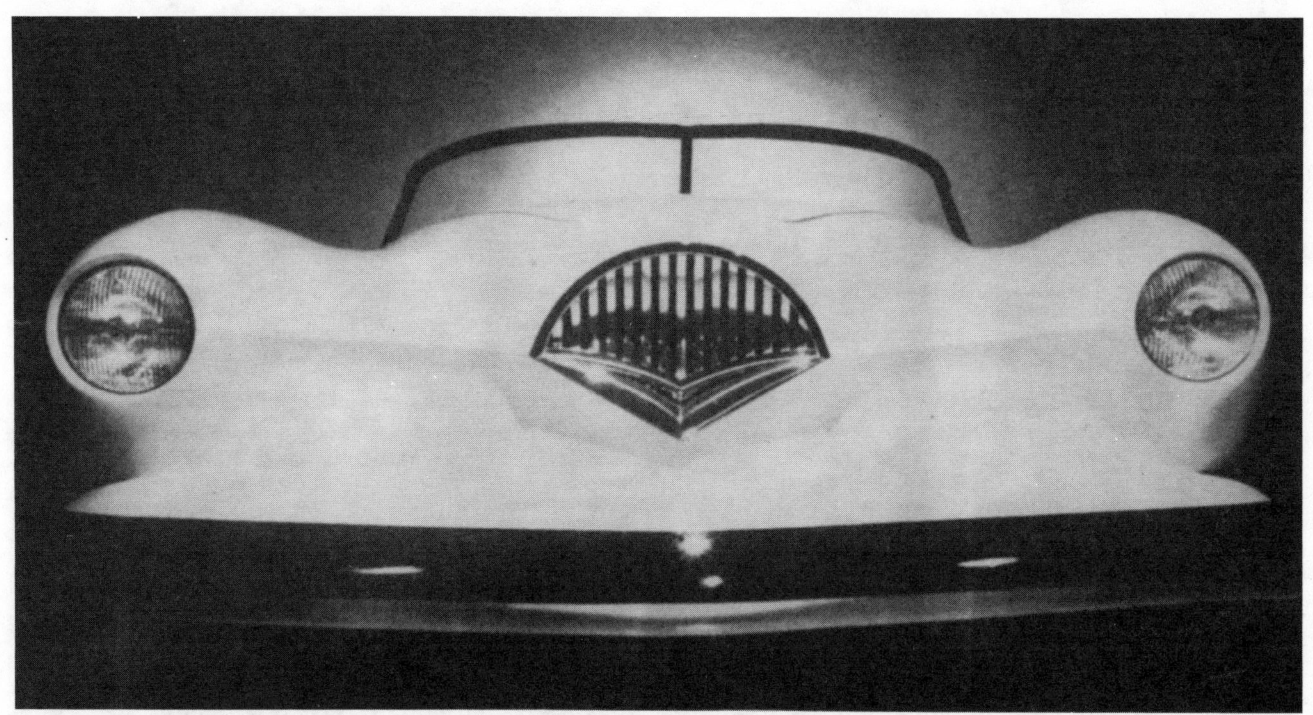

Fig. 7-5. The 1954 Kaiser Darrin had both its good and its bad points. You decide which this grille is.

Fig. 7-6. With a little more polish and a healthier company building it, the Kaiser Darrin might have given the early Thunderbirds a run for their money. As it was, the Darrin was dead shortly after the first Birds made the scene.

140 hourses at 3900 rpm. This means that Kaiser handling, excellent from the very earliest models, is now matched by a performance powerplant.

The last Kaiser I'll look at is also the most interesting, and the most desirable: the Kaiser Darrin.

Exactly 435 Kaiser Darrins were built. More than half of those are probably still around today. Made of fiberglass, the Kaiser Darrin is often compared to its contemporary, the Chevrolet Corvette. In fact, it's not much like the Vette. If anything, it's like the early Ford Thunderbirds; more a boulevard cruiser than a sports car. One thing for sure, this machine is a dreamboat. It also happens to be a certified milestone (Fig. 7-5).

Looking at the design of the car, it is difficult to make an all encompassing statement. Some elements of the car's design are breathtaking. Others can only be described as stupid. From the side, the car appears every bit the Corvette's and Thunderbird's equal. The rear view is good but could have been improved considerably by proper taillights. A ridiculous little (no, make that tiny) grille up front creates a three point look and, for my money, ruins the entire nose. A couple of clever touches are doors that slide into the front fenders and a three position convertible top.

Standard equipment includes a 161 cube, 90 horsepower six and a three-speed on the floor. A fair share of Kaiser Darrins were also built with the optional supercharger. Most have overdrive. (It provides an interesting side note that the last few Kaiser Darrins were fitted with Cadillac V-8's.) The whole thing rides on a 100-inch wheelbase. The enthusiast who puts one through its paces will be pleased with a top speed of over 100 and fuel economy of around 25 mpg.

Available Kaiser Darrin colors in 1954 were white, red, yellow and light green. Seat belts and wire wheels, which should have been standard equipment, were high dollar options. Base price new was $3,668. It'll cost a little more than that to pick one up today (Fig. 7-6).

In 1955 Kaiser was all but dead. The Manhattan was produced and sold, but the '55's are identical to the '54's.

The plan of Joe Frazier and Henry Kaiser to build and sell millions of automobiles to a car-hungry country had not failed, it had just not succeeded completely. Between 1947 and 1955 some excellent machines were manufactured. Every single one of them is popular to some extent with enthusiasts and collectors. The problem when they were new wasn't so much that people didn't like Kaiser-Frazer cars as it was that they just weren't interested.

Chapter 8 Special Interest Sports Cars

Now we come to a very special group of American cars of the Fifties. They are the true sports cars and specialty boulevard cars that somehow just couldn't be fit into the previous chapters. The Crosley Hotshot and SS came close to being covered elsewhere just as the Corvette, Thunderbird and Nash-Healey came close to being included in this chapter.

The cars covered hereafter are adventures: they were built by men with dreams. In some cases, multiple copies were made for the specific purpose of meeting requirements set down by racing organizations. In other cases, multiple copies were made because some foolhardy soul actually thought they would sell.

They were built by the idle rich. They were built by backyard mechanics. They were built by men sick and tired of racing other people's cars. They were, and are, fantastic machines, capable of almost anything, built for road and track.

These cars are not meant to sit in heated garages between trailoring from show to show. These are cars built to be driven. Above everything else, these are enthusiast cars.

CROSLEY

The Crosley Hotshot and SS are the only cars that cannot legitimately be called specialty sports cars. After all, Crosley wasn't a company that popped up out of nowhere for the sole purpose of producing all out sports cars. On the contrary, Crosley was a company that had been in the car building business ever since 1939. But, when Crosley did get around to building a sports car in 1949, it was just as much an all out sports car as any of the others listed here.

(I know it will raise a few neck hairs, but that is exactly why Corvettes and Nash-Healeys are listed elsewhere. Both of those truly fine machines were intended to be sporty cars, but their purpose was never so clearly defined. They *became* sports cars; they weren't *born* sports cars.)

To most folks, the Crosley is a laughable automobile. Why? Because those folks are sadly ignorant of the facts. For the enthusiast in search of a great little sports car that also happens to be a certified milestone, this is great because public ignorance of just how great these cars really are has kept prices down well below what they should actually be. The investment potential of all Crosley cars has improved over only a few short years, thanks to our growing hunger for the world's available crude. Just how much the value of these cars is likely to increase is difficult to say, but you may rest assured that it will increase.

So, let's take a look at 'em. First, the differences between these cars from introduction in 1949 (the Super Sport appeared in 1950) until production ceased in 1952, are microscopic. In fact, there are very few differences between the Hot Shot and Super Sport (Fig. 8-1). The Super Sport is nothing more than a Hot Shot with doors (that's right, the Hot Shot doesn't have any doors) and a little fancier trim. Don't get the wrong idea though; even the SS is a pretty Spartan little machine (Fig. 8-2).

Fig. 8-1. 1951 Crosley Hotshot with optional doors.

Fig. 8-2. Crosley Super Sport for 1951.

The Hot Shot and SS sit on an 85-inch wheelbase. The four cylinder powerplant is a 44 cube cast iron affair with five main bearings. It develops 26.5 horsepower at 5400 revs. Gas mileage is in the 25-30 mpg range. Performance is about equal to that of many new mini cars, but if you deck them out with speed equipment, as many owners did when they were new, the Hot Shot and SS can both be quite a surprise. In 1950, at the 12 Hours of Sebring, one took the Index of Performance.

As far as handling goes, the Hot Shot and SS couldn't be better. With a suspension dating back to pre-WWII days, these cars stick to the road like Juicy Fruit on a boot heel.

If you should end up with a Crosley, don't let a laughing public bother you. Just grin right back at 'em. You know something they don't.

MUNTZ

Two things: First, yes that's the same Muntz—Earl "Madman" Muntz—famous for the Muntz televisions of the Fifties.

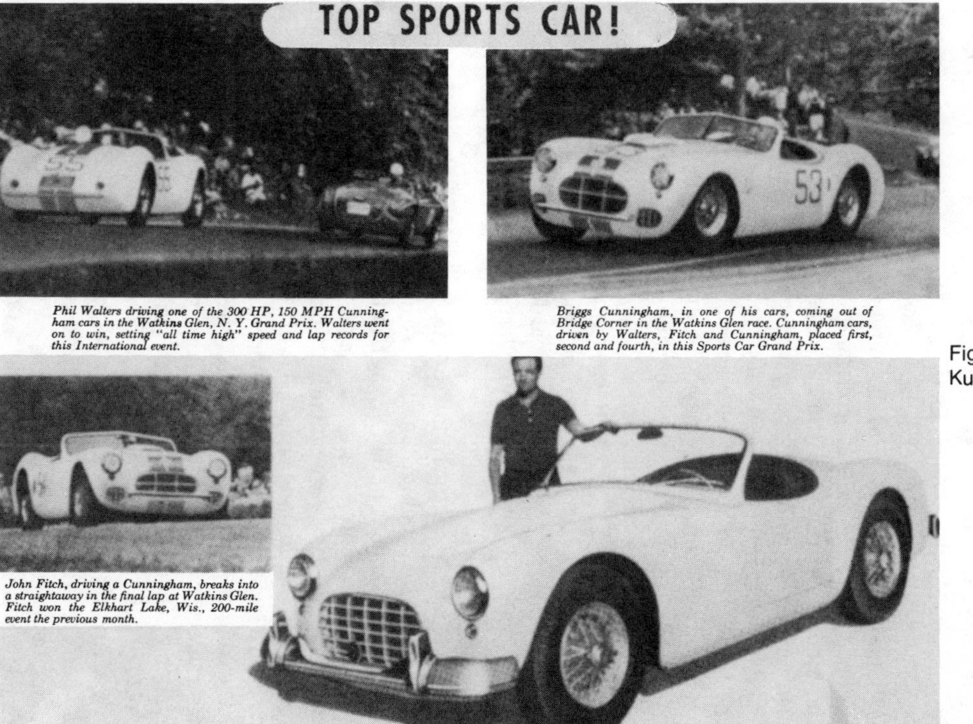

TOP SPORTS CAR!

Phil Walters driving one of the 300 HP, 150 MPH Cunningham cars in the Watkins Glen, N. Y. Grand Prix. Walters went on to win, setting "all time high" speed and lap records for this International event.

Briggs Cunningham, in one of his cars, coming out of Bridge Corner in the Watkins Glen race. Cunningham cars, driven by Walters, Fitch and Cunningham, placed first, second and fourth, in this Sports Car Grand Prix.

John Fitch, driving a Cunningham, breaks into a straightaway in the final lap at Watkins Glen. Fitch won the Elkhart Lake, Wis., 200-mile event the previous month.

Fig. 8-3. The Muntz Jet began life as a Kurtis.

Second, I'm concerned, the Muntz is without question a sports car. Sure, it has space for four and looks like a competitor to the Thunderbird for the title of King of the Boulevard, but power and handling make it an honest to god sports car just as certainly as the Thunderbird could never be.

The Muntz began life, more or less, as a Kurtis in 1949. Frank Kurtis built his fine little envelope-bodied two seater, then tired of producing it and sold the concern to Madman Muntz.

The first thing Muntz did was give the car four rider capacity, stretch the wheelbase from 100 to 116 inches, with an overall length of 181 inches. The second thing was to change the name of the car from Kurtis to Muntz Jet (Fig. 8-3).

The earliest Muntz Jets are powered by 331 CID Cadillac V-8's hooked up to HydraMatic automatics. Later models come equipped with a 336 cube Lincoln mill worth some 154 mad horses. The kind of performance you can expect is roughly 8.5 seconds from zero-to-60, with a top speed pushing 130.

All Muntz Jets were built with a removable, padded steel top. The bodies are something else again. To avoid confusion should you acquire a Muntz Jet, it may have an all-aluminum body, it may have an all steel-body, or it may be steel with bits of fiberglass here and there (such as in the fenders).

The standard equipment on a Muntz in good condition, in addition to the pop top hardtop, includes a padded dash, all vinyl interior, radio, seat belts, console and deluxe instrumentation. Not bad for some 10,000 modern day dollars.

CUNNINGHAM

It would be entirely fair to question the inclusion of Cunninghams in this book. After all, there is only one model you stand a snowball's chance in hell of laying hands on, the C3 (Fig. 8-4). And only 25-30 of these cars, in coupe and roadster form, were manufactured. It is very unlikely that any two are exactly alike. If you do find one in good shape, it will cost $20,000 or more. All of these are good reasons to just ignore Cunninghams and move on to something else. Fact is though, the existing C3's are highly desirable cars; desired by far more people than there are cars available. Owning one is akin to owning a treasure. Finally, in the world of automobile enthusiasm and collecting, everything has its price. And that means they are available. The C3 Cunningham is the perfect example of a car produced in quantity only to qualify for racing in production classes (Fig. 8-5). The C3 was produced for a grand total of three years beginning late in 1952.

Fig. 8-4. The Cunningham C3 coupe.

Fig. 8-5. Briggs Cunningham produced several different cars, but only the C3 is likely to fall into a collector's hands today. The price on one would be well into five figures.

Bumper to bumper, the C3 is beautiful enough to be referred to as a contemporary classic all over the world. When new, Cunningham sold C3's for $10,000-11,000; a terrific bargain considering that wealthy Mr. Cunningham took a $5,000 bath every time one was purchased. That's not exactly the kind of thinking that made the Big Three big. But then, Briggs Cunningham just wanted to race. He wasn't interested in picking people's pockets.

Vignale of Turin, Italy designed the body that is fitted to the Cunningham C3's 105 inch-wheelbase. Its race proven chassis and suspension make it an ideal car for road and track even today. Power is provided by a 331 Chrysler V-8, with a 7.5:1 compression ratio, producing 310 horses at 5400 rpm.

The look and performance is continental. The Cunningham C3 is one of the best all around cars ever made by man.

WOODILL

With all the nonsense being shouted back and forth in recent years on the issue of kit cars, it may come as a surprise to some readers to see the Woodill Wildfire included here in a book about hot Fifties collectibles (Fig. 8-6). If that is the case, it will also be a surprise to learn that the Woodill Wildfire, like every other car in

Fig. 8-6. The Woodill Wildfire. No two are likely to be identical.

this chapter, is a certified milestone. And rightfully so. This car is proof positive that the word "kit" doesn't necessarily mean "not good."

Obviously, the Woodill Wildfire has none of the beauty of the Cunningham C3. How could it, with its square, squashed look and sunken grille similar to that of the TR2 of the same era? What the Woodill Wildfire *does* have is character. Character and a certain kinky kind of class.

(It should be noted that some Woodill Wildfires were sold as assembled cars. This represents a small percentage however. It is important for the enthusiast and collector alike to remember this because of the many individual touches that can be added when a kit is built. The key words are, expect anything, be surprised at nothing.)

The Woodill Wildfire began as the separate dreams of two men, B.R. "Woody" Woodill and Bill Tritt. Woody Woodill was a California Willys dealer who wanted to make a sports car out of the Willys Aero. Bill Tritt, the head of a fiberglass firm known as Glasspar, had designed a sports car body that he was eager to see mounted. At some point, not very well documented historically, the two men got together. The year was 1951. The result of the meeting was the Woodill FiberGlass Body Corporation and the Woodill Wildfire sports car.

The first Wildfire debuted in 1952 mounted on a 101-inch wheelbase. Nearly all driveline and suspension components were stock Willys Aero, including the six cylinder, 90 horse motor and three-speed tranny. The frame was built especially for the Wildfire. Kits started at around a grand, with assembled cars going as high as $4,000.

Wildfires weren't around long before you could also get one with a beefed-up frame and your choice of V-8 engines. With a choice of Willys, Ford and Cadillac engines available when the cars were new, performance varies greatly.

By the time production ceased in 1958, the buyer had his choice of several frames and engines, including one super-powered Cadillac fire breather mounted with dual four-barrel pots. For the driver who didn't care for the removable hardtop, there was also a fastback coupe (for $250 extra) from 1956 through '58. The Wildfire's interior is one of its most personalized aspects. You can expect to find just about anything.

While trying to restore a Wildfire to absolutely stock would be a problem (who knows what's stock in a car like this?), putting one back into good running shape can be fairly easy and a real blast. Here's a car that you can rebuild or refurbish using all the technology and gadgets of a seven year period, 1952-1958, and still say that's the way it should be. If you want a car you can play with a lot, the Woodill Wildfire is made for you.

ARNOLT BRISTOL

Like the Nash-Healey of about the same period—at least in the beginning—the Arnolt Bristol is an international (Fig. 8-7). Like the Cunningham C3, it is beautiful to look at and a near perfect performer. Also like the Cunningham, only a few were built; 130 to be exact. The good news is that you can pick one up now, if you can find one, for around $10,000.

The body is Italian. Almost everything else is English. It's an American car because it was put together and sold by an American, Stanley "Wacky" Arnolt. I don't know why he was called Wacky, although it may have something to do with the fact that he was selling an automobile that cost from $6,000-8,000 to build for a price of $4,000-6,000. (Back home, when we came across a fellow who did things like that, we said he was only hitting on seven.)

At any rate, Wacky Arnolt was full-out car freak with more money than he could count. In 1953, old Wacky made a decision

Fig. 8-7. Wacky Arnolt's brain child, the Arnolt Bristol. Like the Nash-Healey, it is an American/British hybrid.

that a number of others before and since have made. He decided to build his own car: the Arnolt MG. Basically, it's an MG except for a fairly attractive Bertone body. It's a decent car, collectible in its own right, but it's not an exciting car by an measure. A couple hundred Arnolt MG's were built before the Arnolt Bristol came upon the scene.

The Bristol came about because Wacky Arnolt was not entirely pleased with the way his MG innards pulled his Bertone body. In late 1953, Arnolt met with Bristol Aeroplane representatives to discuss the possibility of providing him with engine and chassis parts from their own Bristol cars. Arnolt and his new friends settled on a Bristol 404 chassis based on a 96-inch wheelbase with small, unfinned drum brakes from the Bristol 403. The engine they chose was an overhead cam six similar to the one used in prewar BMW's. But don't be skeptical, because that engine produces 130 horsepower out of its 220 CID. When everything else was in order, Arnolt turned the whole thing over to his friend Bertone, who proceeded to totally outdo himself.

It's doubtful whether anyone could have imagined just how good the finished product would be. A combination of rounding curves and sharp creases give the Arnolt Bristol its special look. Performance is of the nine second, zero-to-60 variety with a top speed of 110.

Perhaps more than any other car in this chapter, the Arnolt Bristol is the best suited to road and track. Any guy who owns one and doesn't drive it is wasting a good thing. These cars are meant to be driven.

In 1963, when Wacky Arnolt died, the Arnolt Bristol died too.

Chapter 9 Selected Driving Impressions

It would be impossible to cover in this chapter every car we have looked at in this book. To do that would take several volumes. Instead, I have selected several different types of cars with different characteristics and put them through their paces. All have their advantages and disadvantages. Of course I had my favorite when the driving was done, but that is such a personal matter, that it really doesn't matter which car I like best. Each of us must pick the car that fits our own wants and needs. One thing is certain, almost every Fifties car I have ever driven was more fun than its modern counterpart. I think it has something to do with personality.

1957 CHEVROLET BEL AIR SPORT COUPE

It has great eye appeal. It's loaded with accessories. It's a contemporary classic. Best of all, it's fuel injected.

Settling into the driver's seat, I'm immediately impressed by the height of the seat and the immensity of the steering wheel. The height of the seat turns out to be pretty comfortable. The steering wheel, well, if you are used to more modern types, you will just have to get used to the giants of the Fifties.

Gas, clutch and brake pedals are all right there, ready to meet your feet. All gauges are easily visible. A glance yields any reading you need. A floor-mounted four-speed is easily at hand, positioned just right for power shifts. Looking out across the hood, vision is good and totally undistorted. With our modern need for practicality in mind, it should be noted that five people could be very comfortable in this car. Nice for family touring.

Pulling out onto the street, the car feels smooth, perfectly suited to downtown cruising. In first gear, the engine is incapable of overworking. At the same time, there is no apparent sluggishness at 25 mph in fourth gear. Without downshifting, a steady pressure on the accelerator pedal is met with sure and constant response.

As I pull out onto the highway, a downshift to second provides the option of moving gradually into traffic or charging ahead of it. I choose the former. The traffic is light, so I let it get ahead of me, then settle down to some serious driving.

The first two questions everybody seems to ask are, "what'll she do?" and "how long to 60?" I won't keep you guessing. Zero-to-60 is a hearty 8.6 seconds, which could easily be improved by the mounting of a 4.11 rear end in place of the 3.55 this car has. There isn't room to find true top speed, but about halfway through third, with traffic in front of me, the needle bounces to 115. Experience suggests that top end is in the neighborhood of 135. A pretty good neighborhood.

At all points, the ride is smooth, with very little float. The absence of noise—except for the whine of the FI unit—is outstanding. This machine is tight. The only rattles I hear are those of the other cars around me.

Steering and suspension are both fairly soft and of course that has some effect on driver confidence. On some winding backroads, I'm aware of slight body lean and some squeal from the tires. These things work well as warning signals of approaching limits, which makes up a little bit for the steering and suspension.

At 110, the ride is smooth, and the driver feels in complete control at all times. The feeling is comparable to riding a hydrafoil across a smooth lake. Dips in the various road surfaces make the car bounce at speed. Return to normal is quick, with no bottoming out.

Basically, the '57 Chevy is a good all 'round car for street cruising and touring alike. And with fuel injection, it'll yield almost 20 mpg.

1959 PONTIAC BONNEVILLE CONVERTIBLE

Again, the steering wheel is big. The shift is dual range HydraMatic. All controls are comfortable. Dials are hooded for added visibility. Visibility through the windshield is less than perfect with some distortion obvious. Lots of idiot lights are in dash to alert the driver to any problems.

Turn the key. Flick the pop top lever and watch the sky appear. Touch the gas. Response is immediate. The faster this car goes, the better it seems to ride.

Power steering carries me through curves with a touch of roll. Not as much as you would expect in a big car like this, though. Power brakes provide sure stoppage. Coming down from speed, the rear wheels admit to a tad of lock up. Naturally, that's not a problem in normal driving. It's just nice to know about. Keeps you from being surprised when you least want to be.

Power response is smooth; acceleration good. High speed in the Pontiac is not quite as reassuring as in the Chev of a couple years earlier.

For those who can't sleep without knowing, zero-to-60 is a flat 10 seconds. You can get to 100 in 30 seconds. Top speed is around 115. Fuel consumption? A disappointing, and expensive, 13 mpg.

1957 CHEVROLET CORVETTE ROADSTER

I'm ready and willing to duke it out right here and now with any clown who says the 1957 Corvette can't compete with real sports cars. Once you are stationed behind the wheel of one of these babies, there is no question about what its true purpose in life is. This is an honest-to-god road car.

The sports car feel comes the minute you crawl into the saddle. You sit low, just a little above the floor, with your legs stretched almost straight out. The pedals are right at your feet without stretching. Your right hand rests naturally on the top of the gear shift lever; gauges are all easily in sight. The left door seems a little too close but this feeling disappears after you have been driving for awhile. The overall feeling is much better than the I'm-up-here-the-controls-are-down-there feeling you get in a larger, family type car of the same vintage. The only things missing are seat belts and some sort of interior storage space like a glove box or map bag.

The 1957 Corvette is capable of cruising around town and tooling down the highway like civilized man and his machine, but they are a lot more fun when you let the animal out.

Response is now: You're over the river and through the woods quicker than you can say "jeeze."

The gear shift has a short—very short—throw, exactly as it should. Too many sports cars have room to play cards between gears. Not this one.

Ride is firm but not uncomfortable. There are no rattles, no feeling of lightness. Powering into some curves, the Corvette displays a trait that makes it a perfect car for road or track. It seems to instinctively take the shortest route through a stack of S-curves without much effort on the part of the driver. The car stays flat while negotiating curves regardless of speed.

Emerging into a straightaway, I noticed something I hadn't earlier. For fun driving, it doesn't matter much, but if you're on your way to pick up Mary Lou for a big date, it's a different thing altogether. If you are over average height, there is more than enough wind passing over the screen to whip all the critters out of your scalp and raise general havoc with your "do." But then, who cares about how his hair looks when he's perched behind the wheel of a machine that looks this good?

Brakes are the conventional drum type. Under normal driving conditions they do their job nicely. Fade comes only at a point well beyond what you would encouter in an average day of driving.

Talk about muscle cars, the '57 Vette will get you to 60 in 6.1 seconds and through a quarter in 14. Before the needle quits climbing, it'll reach 135 easily. To top it all off, no-tricks driving will give you around 17 mpg.

This car has it all. No more need be said.

1957 FORD THUNDERBIRD HARDTOP CONVERTIBLE

With the removable hardtop in place, even the wide doors don't provide a lot of help when you're ready to saddle up. Getting in, it's difficult to tell whether to bend your back or legs first; or perhaps both. (With the top off, getting in is as easy as with any open car.) Once you're in, there is comfort aplenty. (That includes headroom with the hardtop on.) With the softtop up, a slight slouch is required. If you go topless, a full-sized windshield keeps the top of your head from blowing off.

The bench seat is firm, very comfortable and allows for a small third passenger in the middle. Mother, father and junior will have to snuggle a little, but they will fit without too much discomfort. Given the family orientation of today's car hobby, the possibility of fitting a third person in becomes a necessary consideration.

Power seats move you within easy reach of gas and grabbers, as well as dash controls. What gauges and lights there are, are in easy view. Here, I might mention the doctored speedometer, with more numbers added to an unchanged face, that make it impossible to tell the true speed at which you are travelling. This knowledge and a wild guess will keep you within the posted limits most of the time.

The steering wheel telescopes. Neat! And unexpected (read rare) in a Fifties car.

Start the car. The Bird's 312 cube mill comes to life with a quiet, sophisticated drone. Engage the Fordomatic. Smooth is the word that marries gas and gears as the car glides onto the open road.

Putting the pedal to the metal, you aren't met with a surge of power like in the '57 Vette. The power is there though, rising steadily to the desired point. Punching it at 40 brings a jolt down into passing gear.

From a dead stop, 60 mph is reached in 10.8 seconds. Stopping the car is the work of an extremely efficient power system.

Pushing the Bird through a series of curves that range from super tight to sweeping, a tendency to understeer is noted. It doesn't take long to get used to and complete control need never disappear. The Bird is not a sports car, but it performs well. Diving into sharp turns, she hangs tight, staying put. In the sweeps, as long as you don't go too heavy on the gas, she will hug and stay level. (There is no reason why, when rubber bites road, it shouldn't stay bit.)

It's easy to see why early Birds (and early Vettes) are the most sought after of all Fifties iron.

1955 CHRYSLER WINDSOR CONVERTIBLE

First of all, my pet peeve in Fifties cars, that godawful giant steering wheel: In this car, the monster doesn't seem so monstrous, probably because the car itself is so big. Still, with power steering, these huge wheels are a nuisance. Give me a small, three spoked sports car type wheel anytime.

Gauges are in view; dials and controls are at hand. I do wish, however, that the seat would slide just an inch or so more forward. While nothing is really out of reach or hard to get to, I do prefer to sit a little closer to the dash. The shifter is a short lever that protrudes from the dash. This is alright, though I prefer the traditional floor or column mountings. It isn't that the dash mounted shifter is uncomfortable as it is frustrating to have your hand flailing about in mid-air until you get used to it.

Driver and passenger comfort rate a big plus in the Windsor. In the front seat, there is room for three large people without crowding. In the back seat, even with the front seat pushed all the way back, leg room is generous. Seats are soft.

Under way, the car is quiet. Engine and tire noise combine in a low hum. In the zero-to-45 range, it is unexciting. In the 55-65 area, it reaches its true place on the road. The ride is still not exciting, though excitement isn't a quality people go looking for in a car of this type. (If you want excitement, get a 300.) You buy this kind of car for a comfortable ride and trouble free highway cruising. Going down the road, you can easily become convinced that this is indeed a touring car.

On a four-lane highway, I approach a pickup doing about 45 or 50. Just for the sake of curiosity, I tromp the gas pedal down a little harder than necessary. What a surprise! The car downshifts, throws itself back on its haunches, then flies forward like a powerful grey lion after Jon Hall's tail in one of those awful jungle movies of the Fifties! For normal passing, a light pressure on the pedal will do.

In the curves with this big car, there are no surprises. It handles just as you would expect it to. There is a slight lean in the direction opposite to travel. Bumps are floated over with shocks and springs taking the wear and tear before it gets to the driver's or passenger's spine. No bounce, no bottom. A bit of oversteer in curves and bumps and combinations of the two is evident.

Acceleration from zero-to-anything is not fast. Braking from anything-to-zero is steady and dependable. Here is a big attractive car made for sporty family touring in comfort and style.

1959 DeSOTO ADVENTURER HARDTOP

It feels good sitting in the pilot's seat of this rocket car. I'm talking about total comfort; from the seats to the well-placed floor controls. This is one of a few cases where a big steering wheel feels right at home. After all, there's all that car out in front of you and even more behind, and a big wheel seems necessary to keep it all under control. The dash is nicely appointed; glove box, radio, ashtray are all where they should be. So are the gauges that tell you what's happening as you scoot down the road. The only problem I have with the dash is that little bunch of push buttons that take the place of the traditional gear shift.

Not only is it a push button affair, but it's mounted on the wrong side of the dash, over it the dimly lit left-hand corner. As I recall, the contemporary reasoning was that over there, some over-zealous kid couldn't throw you into reverse at 60 mph with the touch of a button. That's bad reasoning. I just don't understand what's wrong with traditional shift levers. In the Fifties though, there didn't have to be anything wrong with the traditional other than that it was traditional, to bring about incredible styling changes. The idea, you see, wasn't necessarily what was best, but rather what was gimmicky enough to give manufacturer A a more avant-garde machine than manufacturer B. If you haven't already guessed, this is one option the folks at DeSoto could have left out for me.

It takes but an instant to find out how well a 383 cube V-8 can work. A little pressure on the gas pedal delivers a lot of power to the rear wheels. All 350 horses go to work right now. Everything you have heard about the stoplight performance of the Adventurer is true. Swift is the first word that comes to mind.

The dual exhausts rumble away as the car rides slowly through city streets. In town, the Adventurer handles surprisingly well. In spite of the expanse of automobile fore and aft, it rolls and weaves through double laned streets with ease. Sudden starts and stops are no problem at all.

I throw my foot into the accelerator hard. The dual quads say hello with a rush, sucking fuel through the system like a drunk finding whisky in the Gobi desert. My back pushes into the Adventurer's Fifties chic upholstery.

On the straights, this machine feels great. Every bump levels out under the four wide tires. After even big bumps, the Adventurer settles suddenly, but not uncomfortably. Rough roads are no problem at all. Even at high speed, it sails around curves. I wouldn't say it has sports car handling, but it certainly handles well enough to make short work of any banked oval that might present itself.

On the esses, she rocks a little. The result is announced through the steering wheel rather than at the point where rubber meets road. In other words, it's a properly suspended car telegraphing messages to its driver.

Testing the brakes, the Adventurer comes up just a tad short. On the first stop, the binders are right on. Some fade appears during the second stop. The third stop is best described as mushy. The fourth stop doesn't exist.

If you're in the market for a big, luxurious Fifties dreamboat that clearly identifies with the decade, look no further.

1953 NASH-HEALEY ROADSTER

First notice is served that this is a sports car on the inside as well as out as you slide into the low-to-the-road pilot's seat. Sitting still, the seat seems perfectly comfortable. (Once you get moving, there is quite another impression.) The big steering wheel seems to put itself right into your hands. This wheel is the perfect example of the old adage, "a place for everything and everything in its place." The Nash-Healey is the perfect place for that big wheel.

From the waist down, you stretch out: way out. At first it seems like gas, clutch and brake pedals are mounted out there on the big Nash bumper. A couple of minutes of this does wonders to accustom one to the race car driver's position. After a couple pedal depressions to feel things out, comfort returns.

Now the floor shift. Where is that thing? Oh, there it is, right under your leg. This is odd. And it is one thing that you aren't likely to get used to. The best that can be said about it is that it works the way it's supposed to. After driving the Nash-Healey for a while, you are actually able to do a passable job of shifting.

Cockpit alterations from the standard Nash include the three-speed, tach and leather upholstery. Tach and speedometer are mounted in full view. Sports car enthusiasts are probably wondering why the Nash-Healey, being so much a sports car otherwise, didn't come new with a four-speed. So do I. The overdrive that takes the place of fourth gear is okay, though. The only problem with the overdrive is that it's mounted dead center in the steering wheel where the horn button should be.

Visibility with the top down is excellent, just as it should be; with the top up, it's not quite as good. When the weather becomes unbearable, top and side curtains fit snugly and combine with the heater to make interior weather down right tropical.

You turn the key and send the dual carbureted engine rumbling to life. What a beautiful sound it makes. As you push in the clutch pedal to shift, you notice that it is extremely close to the pedal next door. In fact on the way down, your foot bumps the clutch pedal's rubber neighbor. Once you know it's there, it isn't a problem anymore.

Pulling out onto the read, you glance into the fender mounted racing mirrors. There mirrors look real neat, but they're useless. Fortunately, the small dash-mounted mirror works fine.

It doesn't take long to notice the traditional sports car ride of the Nash-Healey. This adds some fun to driving the car. Other than a little fun, though, the ride is a plus or minus depending on personal opinion.

Up city streets, down country roads, this is a true road car. Driving it is no simple task. Each bump and dip makes itself evident. You are constantly steering. There is no time to just sit back and cruise.

Steering is super positive and smooth. A sway bar gives the front end a firm hold on the road as you sail over hills and roar around tight curves and through the esses. Unfortunately, the front end is not equalled by the rear so there is a little bit of shift going through tight corners at speed. As long as the car isn't pressed too far, it's as steady as a Russian weight lifter, even at speeds in excess of 80.

Braking is a positive, unemotional thing. The grabbers work in perfect unison, helping to pull you through curves, making sudden stops a breeze.

The 140 horse six provides plenty of power. Give it a hard shot from dead still. First gear peaks early at 30. Second tops out around 55. Third makes this baby fly. Overdrive provides the extra boost to make it soar. In making the climb up through the gears, some degree of confidence is a necessity on the part of the driver, because gearing is so close. Question too long and you will find a very unwilling first where you had expected third to be.

This is a terrific little sports car. For the going price, it is an excellent Fifties buy.

1955 PACKARD 400 HARDTOP

Thanks to an adjustable power seat which moves to a wide range of driving positions, you can't help but be comfortable. The instrument panel has a heavy airplane cockpit influence. All gauges are easily readable. Controls are handy.

The 400 handles well enough, but it has the big car's usual tendency to roll in curves. Unlike other big cars though, this one has Torsion Level Ride which keeps tires firmly planted.

The car will top 110 mph flat out and goes like scat from a dead stop; zero-to-60 in just 11.1 seconds.

The 400's brakes are surprisingly good, with no skid, no lock up in sudden stops.

A lot more needn't be said about the '55 Packard 400. Suffice it to say that it drives a great deal like the '55 Windsor convertible, only better.

CONCLUSION

The sampling of driving impressions included here pretty much covers the various types of cars and periods. When you go looking for the car of your dreams, make sure you drive it. At that point, remember what was said about the different handling characteristics of these cars and use them for comparison. If you can't test drive a car, don't buy it; that is, unless you feel like working.

Chapter 10 How To Buy A Car

So ya wanna buy a car huh, Bunky? Well good luck. You're going to need it. Besides all the good guys out there with good cars for sale at reasonable prices, there are at least an equal number of crooks, charlatans, ripoff artists and just plain old, everyday, down-home opportunists. The big problem is that they all look about the same. About the only thing you can do to make sure you don't get taken to the cleaners is to know something about the car you want to buy and then to go over it with a fine tooth comb. In other words, let the car sell itself.

Previous chapters will help you choose the Fifties car that's right for you. The intention of this chapter is to help you get the most car for your money.

HOW TO FIND IT

First, where do you look for your dream car? There are several choices. Allow me to say a word or two about auctions. A lot has been said about auctions, good and bad. Mostly bad. It probably won't surprise you to find out that I'm not going to say anything to try to change that image. Oh, I will say that there are a couple of auction companies that seem to operate totally on the up-and-up. Far as I'm concerned though, auctions are just not a very good place to buy an automobile. It'll be a long time before any of us in the old car hobby forget what happened when a couple of auction companies bit the dust as the Seventies drew to a close, and who it was that got hurt the worst. My advice is to ignore auctions completely when you go out car shopping.

Start your search in the local paper. Don't ignore weekly green sheets and shoppers. These are some of the best sources. Check out both the "Used" and "Antiques and Classics" columns. You might be surprised at what you can come up with just in the local press. Many radio stations are also now carrying their own shoppers of the air waves, often called "Swap Shops." Listen to them when you can.

Watch the "For Sale" columns in the Sunday editions of the large metro dailies. *The New York Times* and *Los Angeles Times* are about your best bets, but I've heard good reports, too, on the Dallas, Chicago and Philadelphia papers. That about covers the whole country.

If you want more than to just buy a collector car—if you want to get into the hobby—get subscriptions to a couple of the better known hobby periodicals. For Fifties cars, the best one is *Car Exchange*. *Hemmings Motor News* and *Old Cars Weekly* are your next best bets. A number of hobbyists also put a fair amount of stock in *Car Collector* and *Cars and Parts*. All of these publications are good places to shop through the classifieds. If you have no need for a subscription, all can be found at larger newstands. (Addresses for these and other publications are listed in the appendices at the back of this book.)

Back in the days when fuel was cheap, a lot of folks went out to find cars by the method known as hunt-and-peck. They cruised the city streets and back country roads just to see what kind of vintage tin they could turn up. This is still the most fun kind of car shopping. It's not very practical anymore, though and only the high rollers can afford it on any but the rarest of occasions.

A final, and possibly the best, place to car shop is in club magazines and newsletters. This route is best taken if you have a very specific car in mind. Generally you have to be a member of a club to get its newsletter, but if you have a specific interest, you would probably want to join anyway. Clubs are an excellent place to find a car, especially one make/marque clubs. Here you will find the car you want, generally advertised honestly and for a fair price. In fact, the money you can save by buying a car from within a club can pay for membership in the club over and over. (A list of clubs which were formed specifically for Fifties cars can be found in Chapter 12).

The car you want may also be found on the bulletin board where you work or in some public place; churches, shopping centers, universities, etc. Also let friends and relatives know what you are in the market for. They can be a lot of help. One kind warning though: Never, but never, under any circumstances, buy an automobile from a friend or relative! Making that mistake is like asking for the end of a relationship. Don't do it!

CHOOSING THE RIGHT KIND OF CAR

This brief section is intended to help the person who wants to invest in a car, but doesn't know what kind he wants. It isn't rare at all for a person to want to invest in a car, yet have no idea whatsoever how to choose one. For that person, it's helpful to have some grasp of what makes a car collectible. If you already have a particular car in mind, you might want to just skip on to the next section, "Checking It Out." If you need help, read on.

I have seen a number of automotive writers talk about collectibility. Each of them has his own pecking order for what makes a car most collectible. The order you will find here is more or less a random one, because, in truth, the thing that makes any given car a collectible differs from one person to the next. Because this book is based on some types of cars that have proven to be very hot, it would seem appropriate to begin with those points.

Dreamboats. The head turners. The cruisin' machines. In any era, automobiles that have attracted a lot of attention have gone on to be highly collectible. Everybody likes a little flash now and then. The term dreamboat is identified heavily with the Fifties, because of the chrome, fins and gadgetry that brought new meaning to the word. People like dreamboats for a couple of reasons. To one group, they are a sign and symbol of class. To yet another group, they are nearly the opposite; considered more like pop art and enjoyed as much for their bad points as their good.

Milestones. There are two kinds of milestone cars, those officially certified as such by the Milestone Car Society and those that are not certified as such by the MCS. A milestone car is a machine that, by virtue of its styling, mechanicals or a combination of features, has changed, or at least had a great impact on, the automobile industry as it was known prior to the introduction of that car. In other words, the car is historically significant.

Others cars also may have historical significance, yet not be considered milestones. Nevertheless, historical significance has a great deal to do with the collectibility of the car. The most obvious example is the Indy 500 Pace Car replica, for any year. Cars that are one-of-a-kind have their own strange historical appeal. The first and last of anything built are usually good picks when you're working from a historical base. Millionth, five millionth, ten millionth, 25 millionth cars are often special issues or carry special trim, giving them extra value.

Age is the one sure ticket to collectibility, although in varying degrees. One thing is certain, any car, once it gets old enough, becomes collectible. Most cars go up in value by a jump when they reach 25, simply because that is the point at which they are considered antiques. Keep in mind though that a car that has been barking for 24 years, doesn't automatically shed its dog fur and double in value at the moment it turns 25. Basically, age is not a very good thing to bank on.

Tied in with the age is the element of current condition. Yes, condition is an important factor in the value of any collectible car, but even the dullest automobiles in existence gain a certain value with the right combination of age and condition. A car with extremely low mileage or in near perfect original condition has a special attraction all its own.

Cars with extremely good reputations for economy and dependability are on some occasions sought after for those reasons alone. Considering our current energy situation, this could become increasingly significant.

There are certain cars that have become popular because of the publicity they have gotten. A numer of different cars fall into this category. At opposite ends of the spectrum are Corvettes and Edsels, yet they have something in common. That is, that one important element in their popularity is the public attention, notoriety if you must, they attract through constant coverage in the general and hobby press and the activities of a strong club. It has not been unheard of for the media to make a car a superstar overnight. If you doubt the power of a strong club, consider for a moment not only Edsel, but the Corvair as well.

Certain specific cars are desirable to some enthusiasts and collectors because of people and things connected with them. Take for instance the Humphrey Bogart Thunderbird, Elvis Presley's Lincoln Continental or the cars used in the movie "American Graffitti." As far as I'm concerned, this is the worst reason of all to buy a car. It's purely an ego trip. There is nothing all that special about these cars, and they aren't more enjoyable to own just because they're famous or infamous. If my personal opinion can't dissuade you, think about the headaches the guy had a while back when he bought the famous Elvis Presley Corvette only to find out there's a good chance it's a fake. So who needs it?

One very important element in a car's collectibility is body style. Almost without exception (there are a few), cars with tops that go down—convertibles and roadsters—are the most desirable models to have. Two-door hardtops are next in line, followed by four-door hardtops. Beyond that, special body styles—the Ford Crestliner, DeSoto Golden Adventurer, etc.—will usually attract more attention.

Then, of course, there is the great immeasurable, the one factor that plays on everyone who ever did or ever will buy a collectible/enthusiast car. Nostalgia. The automotive fraternity disagrees on just how important a factor this is in determining the desirability and value of a car. Because it is the factor that is based most heavily on the emotions, I think it is also one of the most important. Who can resist the urge to own the cars that were present during the milestone times in their lives: the first car, the car you first made it in, the car you owned when you got married? These things add varying values to the amount the car is worth in the mind of each individual.

The fellow trying to sell you a car would love to play on your emotions. Don't let him. If you simply must have a car because of the nostalgia attached to it, then at least try to know everything you can about the car and its value before you get out your wallet. Make every effort to keep your emotions out of all transactions.

The ideal car is one that fits all of the above criteria and is for sale at a reasonable price. The more criteria a car fits, the better its value as an investment. To maximize your enjoyment of the car you finally end up with, don't buy anything just for its investment potential. Wait till you find one you really like.

And when you find it, don't get taken.

CHECKING IT OUT

When one begins looking for a car to buy, you hear so much about what a great hobby this is that it makes you sick. Sure, it's a good hobby; one that can be a lot of fun. But you've got to be careful. Literally thousands of guys are out there waiting to sell you a car. Many of them are good old-fashioned square dealers. And many of them are vultures. As I mentioned earlier, they are almost impossible to tell apart until you buy a car from them. Then the differences become glaringly evident.

The only protection you have against the crooks is your own intelligence and acquired knowledge. This is also the only way to tell a good buy. Before you go to look at a car (don't ever buy a car without seeing it), research it a little. Get to know about it. Be sharp. Carry along a list of things to check out and talk to the current owner about. When everything else is said and done, drive it. Driving a car can be a very emotional thing, so save it for last. Don't even bother driving a car that hasn't passed your other tests.

Once you have found the car you want to look at, use the telephone to set up an appointment. Make the appointment for the daylight hours on a day when both you and the owner will have plenty of time to get out the old fine tooth comb. (Don't ever go to look at a car at night, no matter how good the seller's garage lights are. And, don't ever go to look at a car unless you have time to check it out completely.)

While you have the seller on the phone, ask him a few questions. Can you give me a brief description of the car? What kind of condition is it in? How long have you owned the car? Had any problems with it? How does it run? What kind of mileage does it get? Ever show it? Ever get a trophy? (Trophies are a drag but tell you something about the quality of the car.) If you don't already know it, find out the asking price. As you get the answers to these questions, jot them down. Then, when you go to see the car, ask some or all of them again. If the same question gets answered two different ways, don't be afraid to ask why. Ask plenty of questions as you look at the car, and listen closely to the answers.

When you go to see the car, there are several things you should take along: a pair of coveralls for getting out and under; notebook and pen, both to write notes in and to impress the seller; a knowledge of the car's value in several states of condition; and your checkbook, just in case.

Several areas must be checked on the car, but it's not real important which are done first or last, as long as they all get done. The steps I give here are the basics. You may want to go farther; especially if the selling price is very high. Don't be afraid to ask about putting the car up in the air to get a good look at the under-carriage, or taking it to your favorite mechanic to give the engine a closer look. Once you have expressed a sincere interest in a car, any effort on the part of the seller to keep you from going over the car entirely, should be met with a small share of suspicion.

I like to get the dirty jobs out of the way first, so that means putting on the coveralls and taking a look under the car. Look at everything. If you see parts that look newer than others, look at the area around them for signs of heavy wear. Look for signs of rust, welds and patches. Look for evidence of leaking oil and/or fluids.

Check rubber parts for dryness. Look closely at the exhaust system for rust or other damage. Check transmission and (especially) engine mounts for wear and breakage. If you have questions, ask them. If everything passes inspection, move on to the engine compartment.

Once the hood is up, the first thing to do is to eyeball the entire area in front of you. Are there build-ups of oil, fluids or dirt? Are there deposits or corrosion around the battery posts and electricals? Check fluid levels to see that they are being maintained. Lift the air cleaner to see if it and the carburetor(s) are clean. Check belts for wear and hoses for leaks. Finally, have the owner start the car and gun it a few times. Watch for dribbles and sprays. If the engine seems to be moving an awful lot, mounts could be damaged or broken. Before you close the hood, take a last glance around for stains and/or rust.

Now it's time to check things from the outside. Begin with the obvious. Check for rust. Rocker panels, quarter panels and around wheelwells is where rust usually appears first. But check the whole car. Take your time and check it very closely for bubbles that might become rust, and signs of body repairs. Body repairs can usually be spotted by just sighting along the car's side. Waves, bumps and ripples can be checked out by rapping on them with your knuckles. If the sound is more solid in these spots than elsewhere, you have probably struck bondo (fiberglass or plastic filler). Repairs can also sometimes be detected by variances in paint color.

Open the car's trunk. Check for any signs of rust or repair. (And while you're in there, check for a spare and the jack.) Bounce the car at all four fenders to see if springs and shocks are survivors or memories. Look to see if all glass is in good condition. (You should also glance around at the glass from the inside after you get behind the wheel.) Don't forget the tires. They can tell you both about themselves and alignment. Open all of the doors to see how they hang. If they drop or sag when they're opened, if they don't close tight with a solid thunk, you can add a minus mark to your checklist.

When your are satisfied that you have checked everything pretty thoroughly, crawl in and get ready for your test drive. Don't get excited though, before you take off, get a look at the entire interior, including under the carpets. Test each and every seat, whether it's a two or six passenger automobile. Take special stock of the pilot's seat. After all, that's where you're going to spend most of your time.

Touch everything. Work everything. Roll the windows up and down. Turn on all the lights and make sure every light on the car—both inside and outside—works. Turn every knob and push every button. Test the radio, heater, air conditioner and the top if it's a convertible. Does the clock work?

Start the car. Get it out on the road. It may be beginning to sound like an awful lot has to be done in looking at a car, and it does. During your drive test, like in everything else, try out everything. Don't abuse the car—it isn't yours yet—but do take it through a variety of road and driving conditions. Drive it forward. Drive it backward. Drive it fast and slow. Put it through its paces and notice everything that happens while you do. While on a straight stretch of road, check the alignment by taking your hands off the wheel. The car should continue in a straight line. Steer quickly back and forth. There shouldn't be any extra play in the wheel.

Keep a close watch on all gauges as you drive. Work out the transmission. Test the brakes to their limit. Note how far down you have to push the brake pedal before it engages. Give the clutch the same test.

Along every step of the way, speak up when something doesn't seem quite right. The owner is responsible for the car as long as it's his. He owes you the answers to your questions. If he's a fair dealer, he will not only answer your questions honestly, he will probably already have told you about any problems.

Often, an ad for a car will mention recent repairs and restorations. Anyone who makes these claims should be able to show you work orders and receipts if the work was done professionally. If the seller claims to have done the work himself, you will have to take his word for it or not.

The last step in checking the car out is to determine its authenticity. This means two things: Making sure the car is what the owner claims it is and making sure that the seller is really the car's owner. A look at the title should be sufficient. If you are suspicious, ask to see the bill of sale and take a look at the data plate.

MAKING THE PURCHASE

It's pretty likely that you will look at several cars before you decide on one on which you want to make an offer. Eventually, you'll find the car of your dreams. And it checks out beautifully! Now all you have to do is agree on a price.

If you're lucky, the seller's price will be reasonable and your offer fair. Fact is though that virtually all buyers think sellers are too high priced and all sellers think buyers are skinflints. This is why I recommend a price guide to both seller and buyer. Such a publication may not be 100% accurate, but the best ones come pretty close. By the use of a price guide on the part of buyer, seller or both, a note of realism comes to a sale. (A complete price guide for the cars in this book can be found in Chapter 14.)

Don't argue with the seller. State your points and let him state his. An argument will end with one or the other of you telling the other to go to hell, and then neither of you will have what you want. Face it, he has the car, you have the money. Try to deal.

If the seller's price just won't come down far enough to meet your offer, sometimes the best thing to do is just say thanks and be on your way. In time, another car will turn up. Then the fun will start all over again.

Chapter 11
Buying Parts And Services

Hopefully, you will take the advice of one who has been there and buy a car that is in relatively good condition, rather than one that requires a lot of repairs. If you don't have an unlimited amount of money to work with, you are better off buying a less exciting car in good condition, than a very exciting machine in poor shape. Take it from me, you'll be a lot happier.

Now, that may all sound like advice better placed in another chapter, but there is a very good reason for its being here. The more you can afford to spend on that dreamboat or milestone, the better the overall condition of the car you finally buy, the less you are going to need this chapter.

This chapter, though short, is the hardest to write. Not the least reason for this difficulty is that, no matter what I say, it isn't going to give you the kind of help I wish it could. All it can do is give you direction.

The problem is twofold. First, when you start fixing up an old car of any kind, parts are not easy to find. Sure, if the car is a Ford or a Chev, the parts will be easier to find than for a Muntz Jet, but the search still isn't likely to be a party. The second big problem you will come up against is cost. The low cost, easy-to-find parts will add up to big dollars quickly, and the high dollar, hard-to-find parts will melt your wallet in a single blast. Again, the better the condition of the car you buy, the less you will have to deal with these problems. Unfortunately, no one can escape them completely.

Now it is time to check the appendices of this book for the addresses and subscription prices of some of the leading hobby magazines. *Car Exchange, Hemmings Motor News* and *Old Cars Weekly* are the leaders. With its heavy postwar emphasis, *Car Exchange* is the top choice for the owner of a Fifties car. The reason you want to subscribe to one or more of these publications is because of their large classified sections.

Classified ads are the car enthusiast's supermarket. Subscribing to any one of the above publications will give you access to almost any part you could possibly need. Getting all three of them will give you unlimited access.

CLASSIFIED ADS

There are two kinds of classified ads, "Wanted" and "For Sale or Trade." If you can't find what you want in the "For Sale or Trade" ads, you will almost surely be able to locate it through placing your own ad in the "Wanted" column. In almost all magazines, you will also find a large number of ads from companies and individuals that have large stocks of NOS (new old stock) parts or reproductions. Now, it might seem as though there would be little or no reason to look any further for needed parts and services. Wrong! There are a couple of very good reasons. First, if you find the part or service through a commercial hobby publication, you are more often than not going to pay dearly for it. Second, you will most likely be dealing through the mails, and that can lead to all sorts of problems. In addition to the obvious problem of loss and damage one often encounters in dealings with the postal service, there is also a lot of misrepresentation. You will find that most of the people you deal with will be honest and fair, but there are enough bad guys out there that you must be careful in each and every transaction.

SWAP MEET

Another place in which you will encounter premium prices and a fair share of black hats, along with those necessary parts and services, is the swap meet. Swap meets are flea markets for automobile enthusiasts. They are held all over the country, all year round, though most take place between March and November. They range in size from the small local club swaps, with anywhere from five to 25 vendors, to the huge AACA (Antique Automobile Club of America) Eastern Fall Meet, where literally thousands of vendors peddle their wares.

The nice thing about a swap meet is that you can see a part before you buy it; or in the case of a service, you can see the kind of work a fellow does. And, if the price seems a bit out of line you can barter with the seller right there and then. (By the way, the swap meet can sometimes be a good place to buy a car for these very same reasons.)

CLUB NEWSLETTER

An excellent source of parts and services that too many collector car owners ignore is the club newsletter. Virtually every club has a newsletter. All you have to do to get it is join the club. I would recommend that anyone purchasing a collector/enthusiast car join a car club right away. In the newsletter, you will not only find a selection of classified ads, but also a fair amount of other technical information that will help you along in the purchase of goods and services. One final thing you will find in club newsletters are the names of specialists who work on cars like yours. These specialists often advertise nowhere else.

As soon as you buy your car, you should start looking in the commercial periodicals, at the swap meets and in your club newsletter for repair manuals and catalogs that include information on your car. The parts and service manuals for your specific car come first, after which, you should start looking for catalogs that pertain. These books will not only give you much needed information on servicing your vehicle, but they will provide you with part numbers. The longer you have your car, the more important you will realize it is to have numbers.

When you have numbers, you will be able to lead a much more detailed, and usually successful, search for elusive parts.

One thing you should always keep in mind is that, if you have a part number, you may be able to go down to the local automotive parts store and buy it off the shelf. Same goes for the local dealer's service department if you own a car that's still in production; GM, Ford, Chrysler, or AMC products. Many people in the car hobby ignore this avenue, assuming that no one carries parts for older cars. Give it a try at any rate. And if one place doesn't have what you're looking for, go to another. Most dealers only carry a limited number of items in each part category.

Make friends with the fellows in parts stores and service departments. Buy from them regularly. When possible, deal with the same person in each store. Ask for help when you need it and be appreciative when you get it. Eventually you will find that your counterman will go out of his way to help you out. He will have taken a personal interest in you and your car. Remember too, most parts stores give discounts to regular customers.

Dealing with the cars of the Fifties, as we are, parts and services are still pretty much available. Neither has escalated to the point—except in a few rare cases—of the cars of previous decades, where just thinking about repairs costs you money. Get that machine in shape and keep it there though, the Fifties get farther away each day.

Chapter 12

Car Clubs

Clubs have been mentioned off and on in previous chapters. Perhaps that means enough has been said about them, but I don't think so. In my opinion, you can't say enough about clubs. They are the heart and soul of the hobby. One man alone can buy a car, fix it up, enjoy it and eventually sell it. Belonging to a club isn't a necessity. On the other hand, if you do belong to a club, fixing it up will be a lot easier, you'll enjoy it 10 times as much and, when you're ready to sell it, your fellow club members will make up a most select group of prospective buyers.

ADVANTAGES

The advantages of belonging to a club when it comes to fixing up a car have been mentioned to some extent in the previous chapter. In addition to what already has been said, there is physical help. A club and its chapters will put you in touch with others of the same interests in the same area. Along the same line, belonging will make you an automatic part of club swap meets.

Clubs help you enjoy your car more in a number of ways. Each club has its own group of activities—organized and otherwise. Some of the things clubs do for fun are shows, tours, picnics, rallies, banquets, hill climbs, races and just plain old parties. In addition to all that, major national clubs hold an annual national meet where anything and everything can, and usually does, happen.

Probably the biggest advantage in belonging to a club is one that's already been pointed out: receiving the various club publications. So important is this that a club without any publication is not worth joining. Virtually all clubs have a newsletter. Some also put out a magazine. Many of them issue service bulletins for member cars. A few even publish an occasional book. Club publications inform you on technical and historic aspects of member cars as well as keeping you up to date on hobby news and doings and acquainting you with your fellow club members. Generally, the classified sections in club publications are free to members.

I could go on and on and never say what a big, important part clubs play in the car hobby. Suffice it to say that, if you own a hobby car and don't belong to a hobby club, you are missing a whole lot.

A SELECTED LIST OF CLUBS

Multi-Make Clubs

Antique Automobile Club of America
501 West Governor Rd.
Hershey, PA 19703
Classic Car Club of America
PO Box 443
Madison, NJ 07940
Contemporary Historical Vehicle Association
PO Box 40, Dept. TAB
Antioch, TN 37013
Customized Cars of America
PO Box 465
Norfolk, VA 23501
The Milestone Car Society
PO Box 0850, Dept. TAB
Indianapolis, IN 46250
National Panel Delivery Club
735 Pleasant St.
Highland Springs, VA 23075
The National Sport Custom Registry, Inc.
1306 Brick St.
Burlington, IA 52601
National Street Rod Association
3041 Getwell
Memphis, TN 38118
National Woodie Club
5522 W. 140th St.
Hawthorne, CA 90250
Pace Car Society
1490 Overhill Road
Golden, CO 80401
Sedan Deliveries Ltd.
48 Church St.
Slatersville, RI 02876
Sports Car Collectors Society of America
1029 Loyalist Ct.
Mt. Pleasant, SC 29464

U.S.A. Convertible Club
PO Box 423
Annapolis, MD 21404
Y-City Custom Cars
417 N. 11th St.
Newark, OH 43055
Vintage Sports Car Club of America
170 Wetherill Rd.
Garden City, NY 11530

ONE MAKE CLUBS

American Motors

American Motors Owners Association
1615 Purvis Ave.
Janesville, WI 53545
Badger State AMX/AMC Club, Inc.
4136 S. 112th St.
Greenfield, WI 53228

Arnolt Bristol

Arnolt Bristol Owners Club
3900 Langlet Rd.
Charlotte, NC 28215

Buick

Buick Club of America
PO Box 898
Garden Grove, CA 92642
Gateway Buick Club
10417 Liberty Ave.
St. Louis, MO 63132
1932 Buick Registry
3000 Warren Rd.
Indiana, PA 15701

Cadillac

Cadillac Brougham Owners Association
1690 Monroe Dr. N.E.
Atlanta, GA 30324
Cadillac Convertible Owners of America
PO Box 920
Thiells, NY 10984

Chevrolet

The Chevy Association
Box 172
Elwood, IL 60421

Classic Chevy Club, Interntional
PO Box 17188
Orlando, FL 32810
International Chevrolet Restorers Club
719 W. Utica
Broken Arrow, OK 74012
Fifty 5 6 7 Club
2021 Wiggins Ave.
Saskatoon, Saskatchewan
Canada S7J 1W2
National Nomad Club
PO Box 606
Arvada, CO 80001
Vintage Chevrolet Club of America
PO Box 5387
Orange, CA 92667
Cascade Corvette Club
PO Box 363
Eugene, OR 97440
International Registry of Early Corvettes
PO Box 666
Corvallis, OR 97330
National Corvette Owners Association
404 So. Maple Ave.
Falls Church, VA 22046
National Corvette Restorers Society
PO Box 81663
Lincoln, NE 68501
National Council of Corvette Clubs
PO Box 325
Troy, OH 45373
Vintage Corvette Club of America
Box 7
Atascadero, CA 93422

Chrysler

Chrysler Restorers Club
426 Orchard Lane
Manheim, PA 17545
Chrysler 300 Club, Inc.
629 Berkley Ave.
Elmhurst, IL 60126
Chrysler 300 Club International, Inc.
19 Donegal Ct.
Ann Arbor, MI 48104
W.P.C. Club
PO Box 4705
N. Hollywood, CA 91607

Continental

Continental Registry
240 Greenridge N. W.
Grand Rapids, MI 49504

DeSoto

The DeSoto Club of America
105 E. 96th
Kansas City, MO 64114

Edsel

Edsel Owners Club
PO Box 764
Alamo, CA 94507
Edsel Owners Club, Inc.
W. Liberty, IL 62475
International Edsel Club
PO Box 69
Belvidere, IL 61008
Wisconsin Edsel Club
1729 S. 24th St.
Milwaukee, WI 53204

Ford

Crown Victoria Association
RFD 5
Bryan, OH 43506
Crown Victoria Association
14749 Witwer Rd.
So. Beloit, IL 61080
Crown Victoria Club of America
PO Box 465
Norfolk, VA 23501
Fabulous Fifties Ford Club of America
729 Dellcrest Way
Esondido, CA 92027
Ford-Mercury Club of America, Inc.
PO Box 3551
Hayward, CA 94540
The Ford-Mercury Restorers Club
PO Box 2133
Dearborn, MI 48123
International Ford Retractable Club
RFD 5
Bryan, OH 43506
International Ford Retractable Club
2530 Shakespeare Dr.
Indianapolis, IN 46227
Nifty Fifties of Northern Ohio Ford Club, Inc.
PO Box 111
Macedonia, OH 44056
Classic T-Birds, Chevy-Powered
PO Box 465
Norfolk, VA 23501
Classic Thunderbird Association
PO Box 4336
St. Louis, MO 63123

The Classic Thunderbird Club, Int.
PO Box 2398
Culver City, CA 90230
Vintage Thunderbird of America
PO Box 2250
Dearborn, MI 48123

Hudson

Hudson Essex Terraplane Club, Inc.
100 E. Cross St.
Ypsilanti, MI 48197

Imperial

The Imperial Owner's Club
PO Box 991 TAB
Scranton, PA 18503

Jeepster

Jeepster Club
395 Dumbarton Blvd.
Cleveland, OH 44143
Midstates Jeepster Association
4038 Grove Ave.
Stickney, IL 60402

Kaiser-Frazer

Kaiser-Frazer Owners Club International
4130 New River Stage
New River, AZ 85029

Lincoln

'56 & '57 Lincoln Registry
Box 10075
Elmwood, CT 06110
Lincoln Continental Owners Club
PO Box 549
Nogales, AZ 85621
Lincoln Cosmopolitan Owners Registry
2027 Ascot Dr.
Moraga, CA 94556
Road Race Lincoln Register
91 Knollwood Rd.
Farmington, CT 06032

Nash

Metropolitan Owners Club
4 Burnham Rd.
Knaphill, Woking
Surrey, GU21 2AE England

Metropolitan Owners Club of North America, Inc.
104 Marion Court
Jacksonville, NC 28540
The Nash Car Club of America
R#1 Elvira Rd.
Clinton, IA 52732
Nash Healey Car Club International
RD1, Lakeshore Dr.
Addison, PA 15411

Oldsmobile

Oldsmobile Club of America, Inc.
145 Latona Rd.
Rochester, NY 14626

Packard

The Packard Caribbean Roster
PO Box 765
Huntington Beach, CA 92648
The Packard Club
PO Box 2808
Oakland, CA 94618
Packards International Motor Car Club
302 French St.
Santa Ana, CA 92701

Pontiac

Pontiac-Oakland Club International
PO Box 5108
Salem, OR 97304

Studebaker

Antique Studebaker Club
PO Box 142
Monrovia, CA 91016
Studebaker Automobile Club of America
PO Box 5036
Hemet, CA 92343
Studebaker Drivers Club
PO Box 3044
South Bend, IN 46619

RELATED CLUBS

Autoenthusiasts International
Box 31A
Royal Oak, MI 48068
Automobile License Plate Collector's Association
PO Box 712
Weston, WV 25452

Automotive Postcard Collectors
155 Tamarack Dr.
Rochester, NY 14622
Automotive Organization Team
PO Box 1742
Midland, MI 48540
Historic Motor Sports Association
PO Box 30628
Santa Barbara, CA 93105
Madison Avenue Sports Car Driving & Chowder Society
30 Sumner Rd.
Greenwich, CT 06830
Michigan License Plate Collectors Association
601 Duchess Rd.
Milford, MI 48042
Model Car Collector's Association
1311 St. Charles St.
Alameda, CA 94501
National Auto Racing Historical Society
9156 Creekwood Dr.
Menton, OH 44060
The Society of Automotive Historians, Inc.
National Automotive History Collection
Detroit Public Library
5201 Woodward Ave.
Detroit, MI 48202

LEGISLATIVE

Association of California Car Clubs
PO Box 96
Fullerton, CA 92632
Cable
1125 W. Fern Dr.
Fullerton, CA 92633
Iowa Association of Car Collectors Clubs
Box 489
Marion, IA 52302
Louisiana Council of Car Clubs
450 Upstream St.
River Ridge, LA 70123
Maryland Council of Car Clubs
11342 Johns Hopkins Rd.
Clarksville, MD 21209
Massachusetts Antique Auto Council
231 Linebrook Rd.
Ipswich, MA 01938
Old Car Council of Colorado
PO Box 16572
Denver, CO 80216
Washington Council of Automobile Clubs
20011 Welch Rd.
Snohomish, WA 98290

Chapter 13 How To Sell A Car

It may seem a little odd to have a chapter on selling your car in this book. After all, just a couple of chapters back, I was telling you how to go about buying a car. The thing is though, once you get the old car bug, it's hard not to get the wanderlust—especially when your particular interest lies in the exciting era of dreamboats and milestones. You may dearly love that car you're driving today, and tomorrow you may just have to own that little, cinnamon colored two-seater you see advertised in *Car Exchange.* My point is this: No matter how attached you are to your car and absolutely positive that you will never part with it, the time may come when you must sell. If and when that time comes, I want you to be able to sell your car honestly and fairly, while getting top dollar for it.

PREPPING THE CAR

Between the time you decide to sell your car and the time you start advertising it, there are a few things you should do to make sure it stands the best possible chance of being sold for your asking price.

Begin with the mechanicals. Give the car a grease job. You don't want to take the chance of your sale being ruined by any squeaks or rattles. Tighten up the suspension if need be. If you have a do-it-yourself car wash nearby, you might want to give the undercarriage a good once over with the hose.

Check for any signs of oil or fluid leakage under the car. If you can, find its source and try to repair it. At least clean the area. If you can't fix it, make a note to tell the prospective buyer about it. If you don't tell him, he will probably find out anyway and you could lose the sale because of it. Be honest about problems with the car in this and any other areas. By doing so, you will gain the prospective buyer's respect and take one step closer to a sale.

Make sure transmission fluid is up and change the engine oil. Clean the plugs if they need it. Check all of your fluid levels. If they're low, do something about it. Replace any worn belts, hoses and wires. Get rid of any deposits around the battery. When everything is as it should be, clean the engine. You'll want it to be spotless when people start looking at the car.

Next, take a look at your tires and wheelcovers—and the wheels themselves if they're exposed. Clean and polish the wheelcovers and wheels. If your car carries very small hubcaps, it is especially important that they be nice and shiny. If the tires on the car are run down, put on new ones. Even a pair of retreaded blackwalls are better than bald tires.

Assuming you don't need new tires, get the ones you have looking new—including the spare. Whitewalls can be brought back to life with some whitewall cleaner and elbow grease. Blackwalls can be made to look new again with a dose of black tire paint. Remember that the way things look is very important and that nothing jazzes up most Fifties cars like a set of wide whites. If you can afford it, throw a set of portawalls on your flat blacks. The amount of good this little move can make is immeasurable.

Now step back, take a look at the body of that car. See any dings, scratches or dents? You'll want to get rid of those. And no matter how good it looks, give it a wash and wax. Looking good isn't good enough. You want that car to look its best. Is all the glass uncracked and unbroken? If not, get it fixed. Check all the exterior lights. Replace those that don't work.

Open the trunk. It should be completely clean and dry. Is there a trunk courtesy light? See that it works. Inside the trunk should be one spare, fully inflated; jack and jack handle and tool kit if one goes with the car. There shouldn't be anything in the trunk or anywhere else that you don't intend to sell with the car. Remember that little touches can make the sale. If you have always carried a picnic blanket in the trunk, and it looks good there, leave it there.

When everything else is right, move on to the interior. This is the part of the car more than any other that can make or break the sale. You know what that means. That's right, not a speck of dirt in sight. Clean the carpet and upholstery. Sew up any holes. If the seats are worn or badly stained, put on seat covers. If the carpet is worn, buy a couple of cheap mats to throw down both front and back. Clean up all the door panels. Polish the dash. Make the inside of that automobile look as new as you possibly can. Anything that doesn't work should be made to work. A dome light and glove box light that work will be especially impressive. It would seem to be a never ending source of amazement that old car clocks can still work after 20 and 30 years, so if yours works, set it at the correct time; to the minute. If it doesn't work, set it at three, six or nine o'clock. Setting it at 12 will hide one of the hands.

Replace blown fuses. Put dangling wires back up under the dash. Set the radio to a station that plays well. If you can get a station that plays classical music, or at least muzak, all the better. Don't let anybody kid you, psychology plays a big part in the purchase of an automobile.

Take one last look. If you're having strong second thoughts about selling, then you know it's ready. (Who knows, once you have the thing back in shape, maybe you'll decide not to sell it.)

PLACING THE AD

You will want to place ads in several places. Assuming you have followed my advice and joined a club, you will want to take advantage of your club newsletter or magazine by placing an ad where others you know to be interested in the kind of car you have will see it. This is a captive audience.

You will also want to place ads in the hobby press. Each publication has its special advantages. *Car Exchange* caters to the postwar—especially Fifties— car enthusiast. *Old Cars* is weekly in frequency. *Hemmings Motor News* has the largest circulation. If you can afford it, an ad in all three will let virtually all hobbyists know about your car. Take note though, ads placed in several periodicals for the same item should be timed to appear at the same time. The various advertising staffs will help you with this. They are also the ones who will send you rate cards and ad forms for their publications. Put an ad in the Sunday paper for the biggest town nearby. Every area has shoppers, many of which offer free classifieds. Take advantage of them. Same goes for local radio swap shops.

It's always a good idea to double plant ads. For instance, in the hobby press, you might list your 1957 Corvette in both "Chevrolet" and "Sports and Foreign Cars." In the local press, run an ad under "Used Cars" and one under "Antiques and Classics" or "Collectibles." It's hard to tell where the guy who is going to buy your car will look first. If you double plant, you're almost sure to catch his eye in one place if not the other.

Keep your ad concise. Put in everything that needs to be there, but no more. Long ads just make people suspicious and cost you unneeded dollars. Every ad should include the following information: Make, model and year of car; an honest statement of the car's condition; a list of optional equipment carried on the car; your asking price without comment (such as "or best offer"); and your name, address and telephone number. If your ad doesn't include every single one of these pieces of information, it is not a good ad. If it says any more, it says too much. Additional information can be given out over the phone later to those who are interested enough to call. Of course, if the car is a super low mileage original without rust, don't wait to tell it over the phone. That is the kind of extra information that can't wait.

One thing you will definitely want to do, if the service is available where you choose to advertise, is run a photo with your ad. The charge for such service is usually insignificant compared to the good it will do. The better shape your car is in, the more good the right photo can do. Not just any old photo will do though. It's incredible the kind of photos people will use to try to sell cars they have put an inestimable amount of blood, sweat and tears into; to say nothing of money. You want to sell that car, so use a good photo. Don't rely on a snapshot you have laying around. Take a picture especially for the ad.

For the picture, get the car in an open area where there is nothing fore or aft to detract from it. Contrast is important too. A light car should be posed against a dark background: a dark car should be posed against a light background. In other words, don't park a white car in the snow or a dark car against a backdrop of trees in full foliage. Remember that the photo will run in black and white. You won't be able to rely on colors to separate car and background.

Pose the car in a 3/4 front angle. This will give the folks who see your ad a look at more of the car. These kind of shots give the impression you are seeing the whole car. Leave out telephone poles, garbage cans, the neighbors, your family, Rover and Tabby. You are selling a car, aren't you?

While you are waiting for your ads to break, keep the car clean. Pick up one of those inexpensive "For Sale" signs. Put it in the window while you're parked at home or at the supermarket. If you go to any car shows or swap meets, make sure to take both auto and "For Sale" sign along with you. Who knows? You might even end up selling it to your next door neighbor or the president of your local car club.

Plan on being around to talk on the phone when your ads hit the streets. If your price is right and your ad well written, you will be getting a lot of calls. Prospective buyers will want to know what color the car is and why you are selling it. Whether these things are in your ad or not, callers will want to know the shape of the body and mechanical condition, true mileage and gas mileage, the interior, battery and tires. They will want to know how much less you will take and if you would consider a trade as all or part of the deal. They will want to know if any repairs have been made lately (be prepared to show them work orders and receipts for parts and services). And, a few of them will want to know how soon they can come and see it.

SHOWING AND SELLING IT

There really isn't all that much you need do when people come to see the car. Just be polite, answer their questions and show them what they want to see. Don't be over-eager, but don't hesitate either to point out your car's strong points. Be completely honest at all times.

At some point during the showing, you will be asked to let the prospective buyer take a drive. By this time you should have a pretty good idea as to whether you are talking to a serious buyer or not. If you're not sure, offer to take him for a drive and then decide later if you are going to let him take the wheel. At any rate, don't let anybody take your valuable machine out without you being right at his side.

Eventually, an offer will be made. To avoid a mental dilemma, you should have decided long before now what the very least that you will sell your car for is, because the offer you get is probably going to be less than you are asking. On the brighter side, the offer you get is also likely to be lower than the fellow is actually willing to pay. What he is probably doing is seeing just how low you will go. Your next move should be to take a small step down. If his offer then goes up a little, you are well on your way to selling your car. If, on the other hand, he says his first offer was his best offer, and that is less than you can afford to sell for, just say good-bye, turn around and walk away. Don't stop or turn around until he calls you. It won't take long to find out if he can be bluffed or not. If he can't, just keep walking, the two of you could never have come to terms anyway.

And besides, someplace out there is a guy who will pay you what you want for that car.

Chapter 14 Dreamboat And Milestone Value Guide

The value guide that follows includes prices for cars in five different condition categories. Let me hasten to add that it is not intended as a be all to end all. It is not a bible: it is intended to put you in touch with average prices, which can then be used as a guide in both the buying and selling of a car. The prices herein come from several areas: auctions, private sales, advertised prices, and knowledgeable individuals and clubs. They have then been averaged and extrapolated to the point that they should be accurate from approximately the end of 1980 to the early months of 1982. Some semblance of accuracy may be maintained by adding 9-10% to each price on an annual basis, beginning in 1982. There are occasions when prices take a dramatic jump. Of course that sort of thing can't be projected with any accuracy. The cars I talk about in this book are all good bets for steady escalation.

The guide you see here is modeled after the well-known *Old Cars Price Guide. OCPG* has two things going for it. First, it is the most accurate of all price guides. Second, and most importantly, it is based on a five point condition code. In the listings that follow you will see just how useful the five point condition rating is.

The five conditions are as follows: 1) Excellent; 2) Fine; 3) Very Good; 4) Good; and 5) Restorable. A perfect car—a car that looks as good or better than the day it left the factory—ranks a number one condition-wise.

Number two is fine, or to put it another way, the car that most fellows actually have when they say they have a one. If a number one car is a 100 point car, number two is a 96-99 point car.

A very good car—this is the area most of the nicer available cars fall into—ranks a number three.

Number four signifies a good, drivable automobile, completely usable as is. A number four car may show a few flaws, even a little rust, but nothing too terrible.

The number five car needs a complete bumper-to-bumper and road-to-roof restoration, but all components are atttached and operable. There are hundreds of number five cars around being advertised and sold as number fours just because the owner won't admit to it being a five. If you're selling a car, be honest with both the buyer and yourself. If you're buying a car, don't let anybody pull the wool over your eyes.

Also listed here are the original factory price of the car (signified by FP in these listings) and production figures for most cars mentioned in this book. Production figures are one of those things everybody seems to want to know about. Fortunately, they are available for almost all cars. Many figures are available through the manufacturers. Some of those you see here were obtained from the many clubs. Virtually every book available on a specific car contains production figures. If you want to get your hands on virtually all production figures at one time, then you must buy a copy of Jerry Heasley's *Production Figure Book For U.S. Cars*. With some of the cars listed, the best we could do with production numbers is guess. For these figures, see the column marked PF.

1950-1959 VALUE GUIDE

One final note: Listings appear in the same order as they were presented in the book's early chapters.

DREAMBOATS AND MILESTONES 1950-1959 VALUE GUIDE

Year/Make	FP	5	4	3	2	1	PF
Buick							
51 Roadmaster Conv.	3,215	2,000	3,000	6,200	9,500	11,900	2,911
53 Skylark	5,000	3,500	6,500	10,500	14,000	19,000	1,690
54 Skylark	4,485	3,500	6,400	10,400	13,500	18,000	836
56 Roadmaster Conv.	3,539	1,500	2,500	4,000	6,000	8,000	4,354
58 Limited Conv.	5,125	1,250	1,900	3,600	5,500	8,500	839
59 Electra 225 Conv.	4,192	750	1,100	2,600	3,750	5,000	5,493
Cadillac							
50 Series 62 Conv.	3,654	2,000	3,400	4,750	6,000	8,500	6,986
51 Series 62 Conv.	3,909	1,900	2,900	4,000	5,000	7,500	6,127
52 Series 62 Conv.	4,110	1,500	2,750	3,500	4,000	7,000	6,400
53 Eldorado Conv.	7,750	3,000	6,000	9,250	13,000	18,500	536
54 Eldorado Conv.	5,738	2,600	3,600	5,500	9,000	12,000	2,150
55 Eldorado Conv.	6,286	1,950	3,500	5,400	9,000	12,000	3,950
56 Biarritz Conv.	6,501	1,750	3,500	5,400	9,000	12,000	2,150

Year/Make	FP	5	4	3	2	1	PF
57 Eldorado Brougham	13,074	2,000	3,600	5,500	9,250	12,500	400
57 Eldorado Biarritz Conv.	7,286	2,000	3,600	5,500	9,250	13,000	1,800
58 Eldorado Brougham	13,074	1,500	2,750	5,500	8,500	10,000	304
58 Eldorado Biarritz Conv.	7,500	1,750	2,900	5,750	8,750	10,250	815
59 Eldorado Biarritz Conv.	7,401	2,250	3,750	5,900	8,900	12,500	1,300
Chevrolet							
50 Styleline DeLuxe Conv.	1,847	1,500	1,850	3,750	6,000	8,000	32,810
53 Bel Air Hdtp.	2,051	1,000	1,750	3,500	5,750	7,000	99,032
53 Bel Air Conv.	2,175	1,500	1,950	3,900	6,250	8,500	24,047
54 Bel Air Spt. Cpe.	2,061	1,000	1,750	3,500	5,500	6,750	66,378
54 Bel Air Conv.	2,185	1,750	2,000	4,250	6,500	9,000	19,383
55 Bel Air Spt. Cpe.	2,166	1,500	2,500	4,500	9,500	11,000	185,562
55 Bel Air Conv.	2,305	1,800	3,750	5,750	10,250	13,000	41,292
55 Nomad	2,571	1,800	3,500	5,500	10,000	12,500	8,386
56 Bel Air Spt. Cpe.	2,275	1,250	2,250	4,000	8,750	10,000	128,382
56 Bel Air Conv.	2,443	1,500	3,500	5,250	9,750	12,000	41,268
56 Nomad	2,707	1,500	3,250	5,000	9,250	11,000	7,886
57 Bel Air Spt. Cpe.	2,399	1,500	2,500	4,500	9,500	11,000	166,426
57 Bel Air Conv.	2,611	1,800	3,750	5,750	10,250	13,000	47,562
57 Nomad	2,857	1,800	3,500	5,500	10,000	12,500	6,103
58 Impala	2,693	1,250	2,000	3,500	5,500	8,250	
58 Impala Conv.	2,841	1,500	2,250	4,000	6,500	9,750	
59 Impala Spt. Cpe.	2,717	900	1,500	3,000	4,250	6,500	
59 Impala Conv.	2,967	1,500	2,250	4,250	6,750	10,000	
Oldsmobile							
50 DeLuxe Holiday	2,385	1,000	1,750	2,500	3,750	5,500	11,316
50 DeLuxe Conv.	2,772	1,250	2,250	3,500	5,000	7,250	9,125
53 Fiesta	6,000	3,000	5,000	8,000	11,500	17,000	458
54 Starfire Conv.	3,249	1,750	2,500	4,000	5,500	8,000	6,700
55 Starfire Conv.	2,894	1,500	2,000	3,500	5,000	6,750	9,149
56 Starfire Conv.	3,695	1,500	2,750	4,250	5,750	8,500	8,581
57 Starfire	4,217	1,250	2,000	3,250	4,750	6,250	8,278
Pontiac							
53 Chieftain Conv.	2,520	1,000	1,750	3,500	4,750	6,750	
53 Catalina	2,446	1,000	1,500	3,250	4,500	6,250	
55 Star Chief Conv.	2,691	1,000	2,250	5,000	6,500	9,000	19,762
55 Catalina	2,499	900	1,500	3,000	5,000	6,250	
55 Safari	2,970	1,000	2,000	4,500	6,000	8,000	3,760
56 Star Chief Conv.	2,857	1,000	2,250	4,750	6,250	8,500	13,510
56 Catalina	2,665	900	1,500	3,000	5,000	6,000	
56 Safari	3,129	1,000	2,000	4,500	6,000	8,000	4,032
57 Bonneville	5,782	1,750	3,500	5,750	8,000	11,500	630
57 Safari 2 dr.	3,481	1,250	2,500	5,000	6,750	9,000	1,292
58 Bonneville Conv.	3,586	900	1,750	3,500	5,250	7,000	3,096
59 Bonneville Conv.	3,490	900	1,750	3,000	4,250	6,500	11,426
Ford							
50 Custom DeLuxe Conv.	1,940	900	2,000	3,250	5,000	7,500	50,299
50 Crestliner	1,711	900	2,000	3,000	5,000	7,250	17,601
51 Custom DeLuxe Conv.	1,949	900	2,000	3,250	5,000	7,500	40,934
51 Crestliner	1,595	900	2,000	3,000	5,000	7,250	8,703
53 Crestline Conv.	2,043	750	1,500	2,500	4,750	6,750	40,861
54 Crestline Skyline Cpe.	2,241	900	1,750	2,750	3,750	5,750	36,685
54 Crestline Skyline Conv.	2,240	1,000	2,000	3,250	4,750	6,500	13,344
55 Crown Victoria	2,372	1,500	2,500	4,750	6,250	8,500	35,164
55 Fairlane Conv.	2,324	1,400	2,250	4,000	6,000	7,500	49,966
56 Crown Victoria	2,505	1,500	2,500	4,750	6,250	8,500	9,812

Year/Make	FP	5	4	3	2	1	PF
56 Fairlane Conv.	2,507	1,400	2,500	4,500	6,000	8,250	58,147
57 Skyliner	2,942	1,100	2,000	3,750	4,750	8,000	20,766
58 Skyliner	3,173	1,100	2,000	3,750	4,750	7,750	14,713
59 Skyliner	3,346	1,100	2,000	3,750	4,750	7,750	12,915
Lincoln							
52 Capri Conv.	3,665	1,250	2,250	4,250	5,750	8,750	1,191
53 Capri Conv.	3,699	1,250	2,500	4,500	6,000	9,000	2,372
54 Capri Conv.	4,031	1,000	2,000	4,250	5,750	8,500	1,951
55 Capri Conv.	4,072	900	1,750	3,750	5,250	8,250	1,487
56 Continental	9,966	3,000	4,000	7,000	10,500	15,250	1,325
57 Continental	9,695	3,000	4,000	7,000	10,500	15,250	444
Mercury							
50 Monterey Cpe.	1,875	900	1,500	3,500	5,750	7,750	
50 Conv.	2,412	1,750	3,500	6,000	9,000	13,000	
51 Monterey Cpe.	2,125	1,000	1,850	3,500	6,500	8,500	
51 Conv.	2,380	1,750	3,000	5,250	8,750	12,000	
54 Sun Valley Cpe	2,365	1,250	2,500	4,500	6,750	10,250	9,761
55 Sun Valley Cpe.	2,712	1,250	2,500	4,500	6,500	9,750	1,787
57 Turnpike Cruiser Conv.	4,103	1,000	1,750	2,750	5,000	8,750	1,265
Corvette							
53 Rdst/Conv.	3,513	7,500	10,500	17,000	25,000	37,000	315
54 Rdst/Conv.	3,523	5,000	8,000	13,000	18,000	25,000	3,640
55 Rdst/Conv. 6	2,799	5,500	7,500	10,500	14,000	19,000	674
55 Rdst/Conv. 8	2,934	5,750	8,000	11,500	15,000	20,000	674
56 Rdst/Conv.	3,144	4,000	6,000	7,500	14,000	18,500	6,388
57 Rdst/Conv.	3,465	3,750	5,750	7,250	13,750	18,000	6,339
58 Rdst/Conv.	3,631	3,500	5,000	6,000	9,000	13,000	9,168
59 Rdst/Conv.	3,875	3,500	5,500	6,750	10,750	15,000	9,670
Thunderbird							
55 Conv.	2,944	3,500	6,500	9,500	12,000	17,000	16,155
56 Conv.	2,944	3,700	7,500	10,750	13,500	18,500	15,631
57 Conv.	3,408	4,000	7,750	11,000	14,250	20,000	21,380
58 Hdtp.	3,630	500	1,250	2,750	3,750	5,250	35,758
58 Conv.	3,914	1,500	2,000	2,950	5,000	7,250	2,134
59 Hdtp.	3,696	600	1,500	3,000	4,000	5,700	57,195
59 Conv.	3,979	1,750	2,250	3,250	5,500	8,000	10,261
Chrysler							
50 Town & Country	4,003	3,000	5,000	7,750	8,750	12,000	700
51 New Yorker Conv.	3,916	2,250	3,250	4,500	5,750	7,000	2,200
55 Windsor Conv.	3,035	1,500	2,750	4,000	5,250	6,000	1,395
55 New Yorker Conv.	3,869	1,500	2,750	4,250	5,500	6,250	946
55 300	4,055	1,750	3,000	4,750	7,500	11,000	1,725
56 Windsor Conv.	3,218	1,500	2,750	4,000	5,250	6,000	1,011
56 New Yorker Conv.	4,188	1,500	2,750	4,250	5,500	6,250	921
56 300	4,364	1,500	3,000	4,500	7,000	8,500	1,102
57 300 Conv.	5,294	1,750	3,500	5,250	7,750	11,500	484
58 300 Conv.	5,538	1,750	3,250	5,000	7,000	10,250	191
59 300 Conv.	5,659	1,750	3,250	5,000	7,000	10,000	140
DeSoto							
55 Fireflite Conv.	3,500	1,250	2,500	4,000	6,000	8,250	775
56 Fireflite Conv.	3,570	1,500	2,500	4,500	6,500	8,750	
56 Adventurer	3,683	1,250	2,000	3,500	5,750	8,000	
57 Adventurer Conv.	4,215	1,000	1,725	3,250	5,250	7,500	
58 Adventurer Conv.	4,314	900	1,750	3,000	5,000	6,500	
59 Adventurer Conv.	4,352	1,250	2,750	3,500	5,500	7,000	
Dodge							
54 Royal Conv.	2,607	3,000	4,500	6,000	8,500	11,000	
55 Royal Custom Conv.	2,723	2,000	3,000	4,500	6,000	8,500	
56 Royal Custom Conv.	2,878	2,000	3,000	4,500	6,000	8,500	
57 Custom Royal Conv.	3,111	2,000	2,500	3,500	5,000	7,000	
58 Custom Royal Conv.	3,253	1,750	2,250	3,250	4,500	6,250	
59 Custom Royal Conv.	3,372	1,750	2,500	3,750	5,000	6,750	

Year/Make	FP	5	4	3	2	1	PF
Imperial							
55 Imperial Newport	4,665	1,500	2,750	4,000	4,750	5,750	
56 Imperial 2 dr.	5,039	900	1,750	2,500	3,500	4,500	2,094
57 Imperial Conv.	5,523	1,750	3,250	5,000	7,750	8,750	1,167
58 Imperial Conv.	5,684	1,600	3,000	4,750	5,500	7,200	675
59 Imperial Conv.	5,684	1,600	3,000	4,500	5,250	7,000	555
Plymouth							
56 Fury	2,841	900	1,500	3,250	4,500	6,100	
57 Fury	2,900	750	1,250	2,750	3,750	5,500	
58 Fury	3,032	750	1,400	3,000	4,200	5,750	
59 Fury Conv.	3,125	1,250	2,500	3,500	4,500	6,000	
Hudson							
51 Hornet Hollywood	2,869	900	2,000	3,500	5,750	8,000	
51 Hornet Conv.	3,099	2,000	3,250	5,750	7,750	11,000	
52 Hornet Hollywood	3,095	900	2,000	3,250	5,250	7,250	
52 Hornet Conv.	3,342	1,750	3,000	5,500	7,250	10,000	
53 Hornet Hollywood	3,095	900	2,000	3,400	5,500	8,000	
53 Hornet Conv.	3,342	2,250	4,000	5,250	7,750	10,500	
54 Hornet Hollywood	2,988	900	2,000	3,250	5,250	7,900	
54 Hornet Brougham Conv.	3,288	2,000	3,000	5,400	8,000	11,000	
Nash							
51 Nash-Healey	4,063	2,750	5,000	7,000	9,250	12,500	104
52 Nash-Healey	5,909	2,750	5,000	7,000	9,250	12,500	150
53 Nash-Healey	5,444	3,000	6,000	8,000	10,250	13,250	162
54 Nash-Healey	5,555	1,750	3,000	4,250	7,000	8,750	90
Packard							
50 Custom Eight Conv.	4,295	2,000	3,500	6,250	9,000	14,750	614
51 Patrician	3,661	1,000	1,750	3,250	5,250	7,400	9,001
52 Patrician	3,500	1,250	2,500	3,750	6,500	8,000	3,975
53 Patrician	3,735	900	1,500	2,750	4,250	6,000	7,481
53 Caribbean	5,200	1,750	2,750	6,750	9,000	12,500	750
54 Patrician	3,890	900	1,750	3,000	5,000	6,500	2,760
54 Caribbean	6,100	2,000	3,750	7,250	11,000	14,000	400
55 Patrician	3,890	1,000	2,000	2,500	3,750	5,250	9,127
55 Four Hundred	3,930	1,250	1,750	2,000	3,500	5,000	7,206
55 Caribbean	5,932	2,000	3,500	6,250	8,000	11,500	500
55 Clipper Custom Hdtp.	3,076	900	1,750	2,750	3,750	5,500	6,672
56 Patrician	4,160	950	2,000	2,250	3,200	5,250	3,775
56 Four Hundred	4,190	1,100	1,400	2,000	3,100	5,000	3,224
56 Caribbean Conv.	5,995	2,000	3,300	6,400	7,800	11,200	276
56 Clipper Custom Hdtp.	3,164	900	1,250	2,200	3,600	5,000	1,466
Studebaker							
52 Commander Regal Conv.	2,550	1,900	2,500	3,200	5,350	7,250	1,632
53 Starlight Cpe.	2,116	800	1,500	2,000	2,750	5,000	
53 Starliner Cpe.	2,374	1,000	2,000	3,000	4,000	6,000	
54 Starlight Cpe.	1,972	800	1,500	2,000	2,750	5,000	
54 Starliner Cpe.	2,502	1,000	2,000	3,000	4,000	6,000	
55 President Speedster	3,253	1,250	2,000	4,000	7,250	9,600	
56 Golden Hawk	3,057	900	1,900	3,200	5,200	7,500	
57 Golden Hawk	3,182	1,150	2,000	3,100	4,750	6,750	
58 Golden Hawk	3,282	1,500	2,500	3,500	5,000	6,750	
59 Silver Hawk	2,495	1,000	1,750	2,500	3,500	5,250	
Kaiser-Frazer							
50 Manhattan Conv.	3,295	3,000	4,500	6,500	10,500	16,500	65
50 Vagabond	2,288	750	1,000	1,900	2,350	4,250	4,476
50 Virginian	3,195	2,750	3,700	5,200	8,900	13,300	467
51 Manhattan Conv.	3,075	3,000	4,250	7,250	12,500	17,550	131
51 Virginian Conv.	3,195	1,750	3,700	5,200	8,900	13,300	
51 DeLuxe 2 dr.	2,380	500	900	1,750	3,000	4,500	8,888
52 Virginian 2 dr.	2,380	500	900	1,700	3,000	4,250	
52 DeLuxe	2,500	500	900	1,700	3,000	4,250	
53 Dragon	3,924	900	1,100	2,300	3,150	4,750	1,277

Year/Make	FP	5	4	3	2	1	PF
54 Manhattan	2,650	900	1,250	1,850	3,500	4,800	4,325
54 Darrin 161	3,668	3,700	4,800	6,300	9,000	13,000	435
55 Manhattan	2,650	900	1,250	1,850	3,500	4,800	1,290
Crosley							
Hotshot	849	900	1,000	1,750	3,000	4,500	2,499
Super Sport	925	900	1,000	1,850	3,500	5,000	2,499
Muntz							
Jet	5,500	2,000	3,300	6,400	7,800	10,000	395
Cunningham							
C3	10,500	5,000	8,000	13,000	18,000	23,000	27
Woodill							
Wildfire	3,000	2,000	4,000	6,500	9,000	12,000	350
Arnolt Bristol							
	4,500	3,800	4,800	6,700	9,000	12,000	130

OPTION VALUE GUIDE

Nothing increases the value of a car like a few factory installed—and sometimes aftermarket—options. On top of that, they can make a car look mighty good. Remember, a lot of times it was nothing more than a healthy list of options that turned a plain jane into a bonafide dreamboat. If you land yourself a car that already has a few nifty options, great. If you don't, start shopping for some of the ones that turn you on. One note of caution though, if you should buy options separately from your car, make sure they get installed properly. It doesn't take much more than a misdrilled hole to screw up the car *and* that valuable piece of optional equipment.

It's often hard to estimate the value of optional equipment on an automobile because of the wide range of responses it will draw from the emotions of any person. And make no mistake about it, emotions have a lot to do with the buying and selling of cars. To one guy, the plainest car available is the best. When another guy sees a clean, mean machine touched up with fender skirts and an outside sun visor, it knocks his socks off. The prices here are an average of what you will usually see these things selling for in the hobby press, the clubs and the swap meets (Table 14-1). If anything, they lean to the low side. In other words, if you want a specific piece to put on your car, be prepared to pay for it. (Always verify the originality of an option prior to purchase.)

Table 14-1. List of options prices on collectibles.

Air Conditioning	$300
Bucket Seats	$100
Continental Kit	$350
Dual Four Barrel Carbs	$150
Factory Script Exhaust Extensions	$40
Factory Script Spotlight	$75

Four Speed	$150
Fender Skirts	$100
Fiberglass Hardtop	$400
Fog Lights	$50
Fuel Injection	$450
Full Wheel Covers	$75
Outside Sun Visor	$150
Pace Car Replica	$2,500
Power Brakes	$100
Power Steering	$100
Power Windows	$100
Signal Seeking Radio	$75
Tinted Windshield	$40
Tri-Carbs	$300
Vacuum Radio Antenna	$50
Wide Whitewall Tires	$100
Wire Wheels	$400

Appendix A Certified Milestones

The following list includes only those American cars of the Fifties, certified by the Milestone Car Society. MCS recognizes a number of other cars as milestones, but they are not listed here, because they are outside the realm of this book.

Arnolt Bristol . . . 1954-62
Buick Skylark . . . 1953-54
Cadillac Eldorado . . . 1953
Cadillac Eldorado Brougham . . . 1957-58
Cadillac Eldorado . . . 1955
Chevrolet Corvette . . . 1953-57
Chevrolet Nomad . . . 1955-57
Chrysler 300 . . . 1955-61
Chrysler Town & Country . . . 1946-50
Continental Mark II . . . 1956-57
Crosley Hotshot/SS . . . 1950-52
Cunningham . . . 1951-55
Ford Skyliner . . . 1957-59
Ford Thunderbird . . . 1955-57
Frazer Manhattan . . . 1947-50
Gaylord . . . 1955-57
Hudson Hornet . . . 1951-54
Imperial . . . 1955-56
Kaiser Darrin 161 . . . 1954
Kaiser Deluxe/Deluxe Virginian . . . 1951-52

Kaiser Dragon . . . 1951-53
Kaiser Manhattan . . . 1954-55
Kaiser Vagabond . . . 1949-50
Kaiser Virginian (hardtop) . . . 1949-50
Lincoln Capri . . . 1952-54
Muntz Jet . . . 1950-54
Nash Healey . . . 1951-54
Oldsmobile 88 (coupe, convertible, Holiday) . . . 1949-50
Packard Caribbean . . . 1953-56
Packard Custom (Clipper and Custom Eight) . . . 1946-50
Packard Pacific (convertible) . . . 1954
Packard Panther Daytona . . . 1954
Packard Patrician/Four Hundred . . . 1951-56
Pontiac Safari . . . 1955-57
Studebaker Starlight (coupe) . . . 1953-54
Studebaker Starliner (hardtop) . . . 1953-54
Willys-Overland Jeepster . . . 1948-51
Woodill Wildfire . . . 1952-58

The special traits of each of these cars make them outstanding examples of the automotive art. For some of them, it is a mechanical innovation. For others, it is a unique touch of style that gives them milestone status. And for a very special few, it is a combination of mechanical and stylistic flair. At any rate, these cars are the cream of the crop. The fact that many of them were recognized as such when they were new is hardly surprising. If you are about to invest in a Fifties car, consider the milestone first. For most of them, prices are already fairly high, but their values are also likely to escalate more rapidly than other cars of the era.

Appendix B Indianapolis 500 Pace Cars 1950-59

1950 . . . Mercury Monterey convertible
1951 . . . Chrysler New Yorker convertible
1952 . . . Studebaker Commander Regal convertible
1953 . . . Ford Crestline convertible
1954 . . . Dodge Royal convertible
1955 . . . Chevrolet Bel Air convertible
1956 . . . DeSoto Fireflite convertible
1957 . . . Mercury Turnpike Cruiser convertible
1958 . . . Pontiac Bonneville convertible
1959 . . . Buick Electra 225 convertible

Indy 500 Pace Cars are part of that rare breed that are sought after and paid premiums for from the day they hit the showroom floor. They are usually top of the line models and—in the late Fifties—all convertibles. Any of the 10 cars listed above will attract attention, but those decorated to resemble the actual cars used to pace the race in any given year are the real top dollar machines.

Appendix C
Suppliers

It would be impossible to list here every single supplier of goods and services to the car hobby. All it is possible to provide here is a sampling. Suppliers listed here all are possessed of good reputations, but they come a long way from making up a complete list of reputable suppliers. I have no doubt that this list will come in handy at some point. Let me add, however, that due to its necessary incompleteness, there are very likely suppliers of the goods and services you need who are located in your immediate area. Your local and state car clubs will be happy to help you in obtaining this sort of information, as will the Chamber of Commerce.

Electrical

Andy's Automotive Electric
605 N. Main
Royal Oak, MI 48067
Antique Auto Electric
9844 Remer St.
S. El Monte, CA 91733
Generator Services
6996 US 19
Pinellas Park, FL 33565
Rhode Island Wiring Service
PO Box 398
W. Kingston, RI 02892

Instruments

Bob's Speedometer
15255 Grand River
Detroit, MI 48227
The Time Center
316 Chestnut St.
Harrisburg, PA 17101
Westburg Manufacturing Company
3400 Westash Way
Sonoma, CA 95476

Insurance

Classic Insurance Agency
639 Lindbergh Way N.E.
Atlanta, GA 30324
Condon and Skelly
PO Drawer A
Willingboro, NJ 08046
J.C. Taylor
8701 West Chester Pike
Upper Darby, PA 19082

James A. Grundy Agency
500 Office Center Dr.
Fort Washington, PA 19034

Literature

Automotive Collectibles/Hobby Shop
1366 Lyell Ave.
Rochester, NY 14606
Crank 'en Hope Publications
Dept. TAB
450 E. Maple Ave.
Blairsville, PA 15717
Richard L. Knudson
21 Franklin St.
Oneonta, NY 13820
Bert Provisor
930 S. Holt Ave.
Los Angeles, CA 90035
Tibetan Literature
390 Richmond Hill Rd.
Saten Island, NY 10314

Paints

Bob Drew
10425 Pinyon Ave.
Tujunga, CA 91042

Parts

BUICK
Buick Barn
Box 49
Weymouth Landing, MA 02188
J.V. Longrie
Rt. 4 Box 297
Grand Rapids, MN 55744
Yesteryear Auto Restoration
2547 San Fernando Rd.
Los Angeles, CA 90065
CADILLAC
Cadillac Cars & Parts
3622 Pearl St.
Philadelphia, PA 19104
Larry Quirk
2508 N. Avernon
Tucson, AZ 85712
CHEVROLET
Obsolete Chevrolet Parts
202 N. Taylor St.
Nashville, GA 31639
Carroll Hook
2728 Sunrise Ave.
Portsmouth, OH 45662
CHRYSLER
A&B Auto Parts
393 S. Wheatfield
York, PA 17403
CORVETTE
Mid-America Enterprises
PO Box 1368
Effingham, IL 62401
CROSLEY
Edwards Crosley Parts
PO Box 632
Mansfield, OH 44903
FORD
Obsolete Ford Parts
PO Box 787
Nashville, GA 31639
Sam's Vintage Ford Parts
5105 Washington
Denver, CO 80216
West Coast Classics
355 W. Holt
Pomona, CA 91678
HUDSON
Earl Huffman
104 Kayleen Dr.
Bellevue, NE 68005
KAISER-FRAZER
Walker KF
1425 E. Highway 105
Monument, CO 80132
LINCOLN/CONTINENTAL
Lincoln Village
11355 White Rock Rd.
Rancho Cordova, CA 95670
MERCURY
Narragansett Repro and Sales
PO Box 36
Kingston, RI 02881
NASH
Fresno Nash
4017 E. Huntington Blvd.
Fresno, CA 93702
OLDSMOBILE
Sterner's Cars & Parts
RD3
Greenview Acres
Greencastle, PA 17225
PACKARD
Dave Fricken
Box 11
Babylon, NY 11702
Patrician Industries
22506 Port
St. Clair Shores, MI 48082
PONTIAC
Redden's Relics
RD1 Box 70
Lafayette, NJ 07848

STUDEBAKER
Frost & French, Inc.
PO Box 57097
Los Angeles, CA 90057
Weaver Studebaker Services
PO Box 1061
Grand Rapids, MI 49501
THUNDERBIRD
Stan Clapper
Box 74
Clinton, WI 53525
Tee-Bird Products
Box 153
Rt. 100S
Exton, PA 19341

Publications/Publishers

Antique Motor News
919 South St.
Long Beach, CA 90805
Automobile Quarterly
245 W. Main St.
Kutztown, PA 19530
John W. Barnes
Box 323
Scarsdale, NY 10583
Robert Bentley, Inc.
872 Massachusetts Ave.
Cambridge, MA 02139
Car Collector/Car Classics
5430 Jimmy Carter Blvd., Suite 108
Norcross, GA 30093
Car Exchange
The Magazine of Postwar Cars
700 E. State St.
Iola, WI 54945
Cars & Parts
PO Box 482
Sidney, OH 45367
Chevroland Nues
Drawer #720256
Sandy Springs, GA 30328
Classic Motorbooks/Motorbooks International
Osceola, WI 54020
Contemporary GM Magazine
PO Box 1866
Santa Ana, CA 92702
Crestline Publishing
1251 N. Jefferson
Sarasota, FL 33577
Dragonwyck Publishing
Box 385
Burrage Rd.
Contoocook, NH 03229
Hemmings Motor News
Box 100
Bennington, VT 05201
Krause Publications
Dept. TAB
700 E. State St.
Iola, WI 54945
Lamm Morada Publishing Co.
Box 7607
Stockton, CA 95207
Old Car Illustrated
7950 Deering Ave.
Conoga Park, CA 91304
Old Cars Weekly Newsmagazine
700 E. State St.
Iola, WI 54945
Old Cars Price Guide
700 E. State St.
Iola, WI 54945
Old Car Value Guide/The Gold Book
910 Tony Lama St.
El Paso, TX 79915
Picturama Publications
Box 50
Arroyo Grande, CA 93420
Special Interest Autos
Box 196
Bennington, VT 05201
TAB BOOKS Inc.
Blue Ridge Summit, PA 17214

Radios

Blue Ridge Electronics
115 Church St.
Weaverville, NC 28787
Marvin Roth
14500 LaBelle
Oak Park, MI 48237

Rubber

Metro Molded Parts
3031 2nd St. No.
Minneapolis, MN 55411
Lynn Steele
Rt. 1 Box 71 W
Denver, NC 28037

Rust Removal

East Coast Metal Stripping
310 W. Main St.
Norristown, PA 19401
National Auto Metal Strippers
1321 S. Main St.
Salado, TX 76513

Strip Clean Co.
5105 W. 1st St.
Santa Ana, CA 92703

Tires

Kelsey Tire, Inc.
PO Box 564
Camdenton, MO 65020
Lucas Automotive
2850 Temple Ave.
Long Beach, CA 90806
Sears Roebuck and Co.
Sears Tower
Chicago, IL 60684
Universal Tire Co.
2650 Columbia Ave.
Lancaster, PA 17603

Transport

Horseless Carriage Carriers
61 Iowa Ave.
Peterson, NJ 07503

Upholstery

Aftco
PO Box 278
Isanti, MN 55040
Bill Hirsch Auto Parts
396 Littleton Ave.
Newark, NJ 07103
LeBaron Bonney Co.
14 Washington St.
Amesbury, MA 01913

Wheels

Dayton Wheel Products
1147 S. Broadway St.
Dayton, OH 45408
Lucas Automotive
2850 Temple Ave.
Long Beach, CA 90806

Appendix D Some Big Meets

As your involvement in the car hobby grows, the more you will want to get out and among your fellows. Belonging to a club will be of some help. A subscription to *Car Exchange* will provide you with an almost complete calendar of events. Still, there are a few big—I mean huge—meets held annually, that you should know about. Exact dates change every year, of course, but these shows and swaps are generally held around the same time every year. Addresses are provided to help you get in touch with the organizers.

February

Winter Festival, FL. Contact: Horseless Carriage Shop, P.O. Drawer 898, Dunedin, FL 33528.

April

Carlisle, PA. Contact: The Flea Marketeers, Box 1974, Lemoyne, PA 17043.

May

Dunkirk, NY. Contact: Dick Lord, 342 Temple St., Fredonia, NY 14063.

June

Squaw Valley, NV. Contact: Coast Car Collector, PO Box 88427, Emmeryville, CA 94662.

Traders Village, TX. Contact: Traders Village, 2602 Mayfield Rd., Grand Prairie, TX 75051.

July

Iola, WI. Contact: Krause Publications, 700 E. State St., Iola, WI 54945.

August

Milestone Grand Nationals, IN. Contact: The Milestone Car Society, PO Box 50850, Indianapolis, IN 46250.

September

Hoosier Swap and Show, IN. Contact: Frank Litherland, 427 William Dr., Brownsburg, IN 46114.

October

Carlisle, PA. Contact: The Flea Marketeers, Box 1974, Lemoyne, PA 17043.
Hershey, PA. Contact: AACA Hershey Region, 300 W. Cherry St., Palmyra, PA 17078.

Index

Dreamboats & Milestones: Cars of the '50s

by Chris Halla

A 1953 Skylark may be just another outdated relic to some . . . but to the car collector, it's a gem *worth a small fortune*—up to $20,000 in prime condition! In fact, almost *all* of those super-chromed, fin-backed, and horsepower-heavy models of '50s vintage have sky-rocketed in value as they become the most sought-after collectibles on the automotive scene!

From the Skylark, Fairlane, and Bel Air to the Corvette, T-Bird, and sleek Studebaker coupe . . . from the almost-forgotten Frazers, the long-dead DeSoto, and the Hudson Hornet to the Eldorado, Olds Holiday 88, the Packard Caribbean, and other greats of that flamboyant era, this fact-filled sourcebook fills you in on what's really happening in an increasingly exciting and volatile collectors' market!

"Loaded with extras", this book traces the development of the decade's most wildly decorated and enduring "dreamboats" (the cars that caught everyone's eye back then, and still do today) and the "milestones" (models recognized by the Milestone Car Society for their mechanical and/or styling innovations). Includes lots of hard-to-find facts about the design breakthroughs of the Corvette, T-Bird, and Studebaker . . . technical info on advanced features like the push-button transmission, retractable roofs, safety interiors, the super-efficient fuel-injected small-block V-8 from GM, and much, much more. *Plus*, there are dozens of detailed photos and illustrations including eight exciting pages in full color!

Most important, this comprehensive guide shows how to find, buy, fix-up, maintain, and even sell your fifties machine when you find another one you want even more! Here, too, is a price guide that ranks among the most accurate and complete ever published, a round-up of parts suppliers and information sources, plus a list of clubs and organizations for '50s car enthusiasts.

Chris Halla is a dedicated collector of '50s iron and is the editor of a magazine devoted entirely to collecting and restoring these post-war automobiles.

TAB BOOKS Inc.

Blue Ridge Summit, Pa. 17214

ISBN 0-8306-2065-6